EatingWell
SOUPS

SPICY BUTTERNUT
SQUASH SOUP
P.40

EatingWell
SOUPS

100 HEALTHY RECIPES for the ULTIMATE COMFORT FOOD

HOUGHTON MIFFLIN HARCOURT
BOSTON • NEW YORK • 2018

Copyright © 2018 by Meredith Corporation,
Des Moines, Iowa.

All rights reserved.

For information about permission to reproduce
selections from this book, write to trade
permissions@hmco.com or to Permissions,
Houghton Mifflin Harcourt Publishing Company,
3 Park Avenue, 19th Floor, New York, New York
10016.

www.hmhco.com

Library of Congress Cataloging-in-Publication Data
is available

ISBN 978-1-328-91103-2 (pbk)

Book design by Waterbury Publications, Inc.,
Des Moines, Iowa.

Printed in China

C&C 10 9 8 7 6 5 4 3 2 1

On the front cover: Shiitake & Noodle Hot & Sour
Soup (page 185)

On the back cover: Spring Lima Bean Soup with
Crispy Bacon (page 132)

EatingWell®

EDITOR-IN-CHIEF Jessie Price

CREATIVE DIRECTOR James Van Fleteren

FOOD EDITOR Jim Romanoff

MANAGING EDITOR Wendy S. Ruopp

RESEARCH EDITOR Anne Treadwell

SENIOR FOOD EDITOR Carolyn Malcoun

TEST KITCHEN MANAGER Breana Lai, M.P.H., R.D.

RECIPE DEVELOPERS & TESTERS
Carolyn Casner, Julia Clancy, Hilary Meyer

NUTRITION CONSULTANT Jill Cerreta, M.S., R.D.

NUTRITION & FEATURES EDITOR Shaun Dreisbach

ASSOCIATE NUTRITION EDITOR Julia Westbrook

PHOTO DIRECTOR Maria Emmighausen

PRODUCTION DESIGNER Jolee Main

ASSOCIATE EDITOR Lucy M. Casale

EDITORIAL ASSISTANT Nancy Margolin

EatingWell Soups

PROJECT EDITOR Lisa Kingsley,
Waterbury Publications, Inc.

CONTRIBUTING RECIPE DEVELOPERS
Lisa Holderness Brown, Annie Peterson

CONTRIBUTING FOOD STYLIST Joshua Hake,
Waterbury Publications, Inc.

CONTRIBUTING WRITERS Sara Stillman Berger,
Daniel Duane, Kathy Gunst, Anna Thomas

CONTRIBUTING PHOTOGRAPHERS Peter Ardito,
Johnny Autry, Marty Baldwin, Ken Burris,
Karla Conrad, Penny De Los Santos,
Carin Krasner, Erin Kunkel, Blaine Moats,
Devon O'Brien, Andrew Scrivani, Jim
Westphalen (p.11: Anna Larson/Offset;
p.12: Natalia Klenova/StockFood)

COVER PHOTO Ken Burris

DESIGN DIRECTOR Ken Carlson,
Waterbury Publications, Inc.

ASSOCIATE DESIGN DIRECTOR Doug Samuelson,
Waterbury Publications, Inc.

PRODUCTION ASSISTANT Mindy Samuelson,
Waterbury Publications, Inc.

INDEXER Amy Novick, BackSpace Indexing

Houghton Mifflin Harcourt

EXECUTIVE EDITOR Anne Ficklen

MANAGING EDITOR Marina Padakis Lowry

ART DIRECTOR Tai Blanche

SR. PRODUCTION COORDINATOR Kimberly Kiefer

CONTENTS

WE LOVE SOUP AND YOU SHOULD TOO

Whenever anyone asks "What's your favorite dish to cook?" my answer is soup. I know that sounds broad. They're probably wondering whether I do a killer mac & cheese or have a special way with roast chicken. But I answer soup, because no matter what type it is—whether it takes 20 minutes or 2 hours, whether it's light and velvety or hearty and chunky, warm and comforting or chilled and refreshing—I love them all. If you've picked up this book, perhaps you already agree with me that soup has an awful lot going for it. Here are some of the highlights.

To start with the obvious, it's a comfort food. With most comfort foods, though, if you packed them with healthy ingredients—whole grains, vegetables, beans—they'd feel like, well, health food. Soup is different. It feels rich and indulgent. Maybe it's the way it fills you up or the savoriness of the broth. Think of a bowl of tomato soup. You can make an easy one with canned tomatoes, onions or garlic, chicken broth, maybe a little thyme or basil *(see page 35)*. Puree it, sit down to a bowl and taste. It's tangy and savory. The texture is smooth and creamy. It's intensely flavorful... rich even. But it has just a few good-for-you ingredients. That's the alchemy of soup.

Soup is easy and forgiving. There's not a lot of stressful multitasking in soup-making. On occasion, you might have two pans going at once, say a batch of beans simmering while you sauté vegetables to add later. Usually, though, it's all in one big pot (less mess at the end) and can be left alone to bubble away without much oversight. I'll put one on and head out to walk my dog. Or if it's in the slow cooker, go to work for the day. It's that easy.

Soup's also a perfect vehicle for improvisation. Got a recipe for vegetable noodle soup but don't feel like noodles? How about rice instead? Maybe potatoes. Don't have a bunch of kale for tonight's recipe? Throw in a bag of frozen spinach. Want to make something vegetarian? Swap the beef or chicken broth for vegetable broth. The bottom line is you're probably not going to mess it up. And you will end up with a delicious meal. (If you need a little guidance on how to start improvising, check out the *Soups by the Formula* chapter on page 208.)

When it comes to feeding a crowd or a family with a hectic schedule, soup is there to bail you out. You can eat a soup right when it's done, and that same soup can just as easily hang for an hour until a kid gets home from practice. I love to make soup for a casual get-together. I can make it before guests arrive, then its flavors can meld until hunger strikes. And leftovers rule—I package up individual servings to have ready-to-go lunches throughout the week. Plenty of soups take well to the freezer too. I like to stockpile quart containers of frozen soup so I have something for dinners when I just don't have time to cook from scratch.

Why These Soups?

There are a zillion soup cookbooks (judging by my bookshelf, I may own half of them) and a bajillion-zillion soup recipes online. So what makes this one special? This book is different because it's an *EatingWell* collection of soups. We're a magazine brand based in Vermont, dedicated to helping our fans eat delicious food that happens to be good for them. We believe cooking meals, made from whole ingredients, with plenty of flavor and lots of love is one of the essential joys in life. And it doesn't hurt that when you eat the *EatingWell* way, you feel awesome too.

All year long our editors dream up new ideas and consult new contributors. That makes this a very different kind of book from one by a single author. It is a tapestry of sorts, reflecting the best soups we have tested, tasted and published over the years. It includes cuisines from Mexican to Singaporean. Recipes range from Ribollita *(page 50)* by celebrity chef Lidia Bastianich to Matzo Ball Soup with Fresh Dill *(page 202)* from James Beard Award winner Kathy Gunst. Southwestern experts Bill and Cheryl Jamison have shared their Grilled Tomato Gazpacho *(page 32)* and prolific Indian cookbook author Raghavan Iyer teaches us how to make Paprika & Red Pepper Soup with Pistachios *(page 33)*.

We've also sprinkled essays throughout the book. In each, contributors share their thoughts on soup-making. For example, Anna Thomas, a screenwriter and cookbook author, explains how she became obsessed with what she calls green soups, those that are jam-packed with green vegetables, on page 78. Anna's recipes converted us into green soup devotees. Along with her essay, you'll find many of Anna's recipes, and some new *EatingWell* ones inspired by her, in the *Green Soups* chapter *(page 74)*.

You can be sure when you choose a recipe from this book that it's going to work. Each one has gone through the *EatingWell* Test Kitchen. That means it's been tested multiple times to make sure it's easy to follow and delivers delicious results. At least two people test each recipe because what makes perfect sense to one cook may be unclear to another. We also use different equipment, for example both gas and electric stoves, to make sure results are consistent. Once we've vetted a recipe so we know it's going to turn out great for you, we run it by our team of nutrition experts. They provide nutrition analysis and health tags to indicate which recipes are heart-healthy, low-calorie, etc. (Look for health tags on the top of each recipe page.) For more on how we test and analyze, see page 238.

What Does Healthy Mean, Anyway?
When it comes to what we consider healthy, you won't find fads or fuss. We're not into elimination or deprivation. There are no single "bad" foods that must be banned. We do believe in following the best science-backed nutrition advice available today. To that end, we have a team of registered dietitians on staff and a board of health advisors that includes some of the leading experts on everything from weight management to heart health. We aim for a balanced overall pattern of eating. We help people get excited about the good stuff—fruits, vegetables, lean meats, seafood, whole grains, nuts, beans, healthy oils. We believe if you get more of that good stuff, you're going to end up with an overall healthy diet.

So what does healthy mean for our recipes? You'll find that *EatingWell* soups have a few things in common. Often they are loaded with vegetables. See the *Eat More Veg!* chapter *(page 30)* and *Green Soups (page 74)* for some clear examples. There are plenty that are low-calorie yet totally satisfying if you're looking to manage your weight (see *Slim-Down Soups*, page 144). When our soups include grains, they're usually whole—barley, brown rice, bulgur, etc. We're liberal with beans, which bump up fiber. Smallish amounts of meat add flavor and satisfying protein.

We steer clear of the typical soup stumbling blocks. Plenty of recipes would have you ladling up soups that are half butter and cream. While there has been some significant new science on fats, the best advice today is still to choose unsaturated fats (olive oil, canola oil and nuts are all sources) over saturated. There's plenty of evidence that unsaturated fats are connected with healthier, longer lives. Not so with saturated fats. The hitch is that butter, cheese and cream taste delicious. So we have developed ways to use just a bit of these ingredients (which research now suggests are fine in moderation) and still get delicious results. Turn to the *Kindersoups* chapter, devoted to kid-friendly soups, and you'll find cheeseburger soup *(page 99)* and a creamy chicken enchilada soup *(page 112)* to name two tasty examples.

The other big hurdle for many soup recipes: sodium. Getting too much salt in your diet can lead to high blood pressure. The problem is, you need salt to bring out the flavor of all the ingredients in your soup. In fact, salt may be the single most important ingredient for making a soup that tastes amazing. Try a store-bought chicken broth without any added salt or even a homemade one without salt, and it's like listening to the radio with earmuffs on. You get a hint of chicken flavor, but it's dull and hard to discern. Add salt, and suddenly the broth comes to life, tasting rich and chicken-y. Luckily our Test Kitchen team is packed with experts who know how to navigate the line to get a balanced,

flavor-packed recipe that's not overloaded with sodium. (A relevant aside: All of our recipes specify what kind of broth to buy at the store. You can make any of the recipes with homemade, but will need to adjust the seasoning accordingly. Turn to page 224 for more on broth.)

Get Cooking!

Now that you've made it this far, you're ready to cook. Flip through the pages and you'll see the organization reflects the fact that it was put together by a team of editors. So it showcases many points of view, showing off all there is to love about soups. Some of the chapters are based on occasions—soup-swap parties, make-aheads or starter soups. We also organized a few chapters by cooking techniques, as in soup formulas (for chicken soup, chowder and vegetable soups, *page 208)* and how to make jars of homemade cup o' noodle soups *(page 114)*. And we've thought about how we can help you eat more vegetables *(page 30)*, get more beans in your diet *(page 126)*, cook soups kids will love *(page 94)* or slim down *(page 144)*. We've peppered in some accoutrements, including ideas for crostini, breadsticks and toppers. Finally, in the back of the book *(page 222)* you'll find a soup-making toolbox of broth recipes, tips for buying broth and a guide to stocking a soup-ready pantry.

What are you waiting for? It's time to get out the soup pot!

—*Jessie Price, editor-in-chief*

SOUP'S SUPERPOWERS

Soup is good for the soul—and the rest of you too. Here's a look at four of its health benefits.

—Julia Westbrook, associate nutrition editor

It Improves Your Diet

Do you have a souper diet? (See what we did there?) The answer is probably "yes" if you're a soup-eater. Looking at the diets of 10,500 Americans, Iowa State University researchers found that people who ate soup had higher diet-quality scores than people who didn't. Soup-eaters had higher intakes of fiber, vitamin A, magnesium, iron and potassium. And overall, they got more servings of vegetables (notably, more dark greens, orange veggies and legumes).

It Helps You Stay Slim

Compared to people who enjoy soup on the regular, those who skip the slurp are about 40 percent more likely to be overweight, according to research published in the journal *PLOS ONE*. The difference in actual body size was somewhat small—a waist circumference difference of about 1¼ inches—but we think that's pretty remarkable considering participants served up soup just once a week. Plus, another study out of Penn State reported that eating soup before lunch helped people naturally cut 134 calories out of their entire meal.

It Gives You More Food for Fewer Calories

When you include soup in your meal, you're likely to eat a larger portion of food that's also lower in calories. The same Penn State study we mentioned at left found that people who had soup before lunch enjoyed about 27 ounces of food—the soup plus a pasta entree, for about 820 calories—while those who didn't start with soup ate about 15 ounces of just the pasta for about 930 calories. Other research shows that diets rich in foods that fill you up with fewer calories, like soup, are associated with a lower risk of developing type 2 diabetes.

It's Salty, But Balanced

Soup is notoriously high in sodium—and yes, research shows that people who eat soup do get more sodium than those who skip the bowl. They're also likely to get more potassium. This is important for heart health because potassium encourages your body to excrete sodium. So, while too much sodium can raise blood pressure, potassium can help bring it back down. Not all lunches can say that. A homemade sandwich made with ham, cheese, tomato and whole-wheat bread has over 800 mg of sodium and only 320 mg of potassium, but a basic vegetable soup (like our Veggistrone, *page 54*) has about 640 mg of sodium and 718 mg potassium. That's 20 percent of your recommended dose of potassium for the day!

SOUP SAVVY

Whether you're a confident cook who's ready to riff on ribollita *(page 50)* or a kitchen newbie, a little expert advice is always helpful. Here are 10 need-to-know tips and techniques from our soup gurus. Read 'em and cook.

SIMMER INSTEAD OF BOIL
Low and slow cooking—a gentle simmer instead of a rapid boil—is a golden rule for making soup. Boiling causes your veggies to break apart and can turn meat into tough, hard-to-chew pieces.

ENRICH STORE-BOUGHT BROTH Give store-bought broth more savory flavor by simmering it with extra meat (such as for chicken soup, page 211), bones or aromatics, such as herbs, spices or fresh ginger or garlic, for at least 20 minutes. Strain the broth, then use it for your soup.

TASTE & ADJUST If your soup needs a flavor bump, first try adding an acid—a squeeze of lemon juice or a dash of vinegar—to brighten the flavor. Still not right? Try adding salt—a tiny bit at a time, which will also enhance the way things taste. Miso, soy sauce, fish sauce, anchovy paste or Worcester shire also get the job done while adding a hit of umami.

STIR IN A PARMESAN RIND
When you're no longer able to grate cheese off a hunk of Parmesan, hang onto the rind to pop it into your next pot of soup. You'll get another layer of nutty flavor that takes your soup from *meh* to *magnifico*.

COOK PASTA & GRAINS PERFECTLY Even after the stove is off, heat from the soup continues to soften ingredients. If you're planning leftovers, you can keep pasta and grains from turning to mush by cooking them in soup for a touch less than the package directions. Or cook them separately and stir into the soup just before serving for the perfect texture.

EMPLOY THE WHOLE VEGETABLE Stems and tops from veggies like broccoli, chard and leeks become tender when cooked and you'll get all those extra nutrients and fiber while reducing food waste. See this tip in action in the Green Curry Soup on page 83.

THICKEN WITH STALE BREAD, BEANS OR MASHED POTATOES When stirred into soup, stale bread, mashed beans and mashed potatoes cook down to create a creamy, rich texture, all without adding cream. It's also a great way to use up leftovers.

RINSE CANNED BEANS Here's an instant way to make canned beans healthier before adding them to soup: rinse them. Giving beans a cold shower reduces sodium by a third.

USE THE SOAKING LIQUID Dried chiles and mushrooms have concentrated flavor that ends up in the rehydrating liquid. Strain this flavorful soaking liquid through a fine-mesh sieve or cheesecloth and use it in soup for an extra hit of flavor, as we do on page 29.

ADD SOFT HERBS AT THE END Fresh soft herbs, such as basil, parsley and cilantro, lose their flavor when cooked too long. To preserve their essence, add them just before serving. Hardier herbs, like sage and rosemary, can cook longer and be added earlier.

TOOLS FOR SOUP

Technically, all you need is a pot and a spoon. But cooking is much easier and faster with the right equipment. Nab these essentials for making soup and get stirring, whizzing and slurping.

LARGE POT A large pot (sometimes called a Dutch oven) with a wide, heavy bottom is the workhorse when it comes to making soup. Pick a heavy pot that holds at least 4 quarts and is made of stainless steel or enameled cast iron, such as a Le Creuset, to make sure your soup cooks evenly and doesn't burn on the bottom.

STOCKPOT Typically much taller than a large pot, stockpots can hold up to a whopping 20 quarts. The tall sides prevent too much liquid from evaporating during the long cooking times needed to make a rich-tasting broth. They're also necessary for making extra-large batches of soup.

LONG-HANDLED WOODEN SPOON Unlike metal, this tool stays cool as you stir and won't scratch your pot, especially if you have any bits stuck to the bottom you need to scrape up.

SOUP SKIMMER This flat, circular strainer is particularly important when making stock to skim froth and any unwanted bits off the surface.

LADLE With a deep, rounded bottom, a large soup ladle means fewer trips from pot to bowl. If you're watching portion size, purchase one that has cup measures inside the ladle so you know how much you're eating. If your ladle isn't labeled, transfer a full scoop into a measuring cup so you know how much it holds.

CHINOIS OR CHINA CAP STRAINER Serious soup-makers need serious sieves. These large conical strainers are made of very fine mesh or perforated metal and are deeper than a typical colander, so you can really load them up to strain broths or make soups smooth.

HIGH-POWERED BLENDER While any blender will work, high-powered blenders, such as a Vitamix or Oster Versa, create the smoothest soups. The stronger motors pulverize ingredients quicker and whip air into the mixture, creating a light and fluffy texture. Plus, new models often have an oversized pitcher, so you may not have to puree in batches.

IMMERSION BLENDER This tool lets you puree directly in the pot so you don't risk a mess when transferring hot soup to a blender. Plus, most immersion blender blades snap off and go straight into the dishwasher, making cleanup a breeze.

MICROPLANE These thin graters are perfect for adding a super-fine finishing touch of hard cheese or citrus zest to soup. Use for grating garlic, ginger and nutmeg as well.

SLOW COOKER It's hard to beat the convenience of a slow cooker. Beans, lentils, tough cuts of meat and root vegetables all turn to tender morsels, no stirring required. Be sure to purchase one that automatically switches to "warm" when it's finished.

STORAGE Most soup recipes are easily doubled and some even taste better as leftovers. For storing and transporting soup, we like glass containers with lids that snap to form a tight seal. Glass containers allow you to see what's inside, can go in the microwave and last longer than plastic. Look for containers with BPA-free lids.

MARYLAND OYSTER STEW
P.18

START WITH SOUP

These days, multi-course meals tend to be left to the realm of restaurants. But for the holidays, a special birthday or some other celebratory occasion, a menu that starts with a beautiful, light bowl of soup, say oyster stew, may be just the thing to set the tone of the evening.

MARYLAND OYSTER STEW

This delicate oyster soup recipe sets the tone for celebration. We made this stew healthier by primarily using low-fat milk with just the right amount of cream for richness. Serve with crusty bread to sop up all the delicious bits at the bottom of the bowl. *(Photo: page 16.)*

3 tablespoons butter

2 cups diced white onion

1 cup diced celery, plus ¼ cup chopped celery leaves, divided

2 pints shucked oysters, liquid reserved

¾ teaspoon kosher salt

½ teaspoon paprika

3½ cups low-fat milk

½ cup heavy cream

3 dashes hot sauce

Ground pepper to taste

2 tablespoons snipped fresh chives

1. Heat butter in a large saucepan over medium heat until melted. Add onion and celery, reduce heat to medium-low and cook, stirring occasionally, until translucent and very tender but not browned, 25 to 30 minutes.

2. Meanwhile, cut oysters in half or quarters, depending on size. Pour the oyster liquid through a fine-mesh sieve to strain out any grit.

3. Stir salt and paprika into the vegetables and cook, stirring, for 1 minute more. Add the strained oyster liquid, milk, cream and hot sauce. Increase heat to high and bring to a boil.

4. Reduce heat to a simmer and gently add the oysters. Cook just until their edges begin to curl, 2 to 3 minutes. Remove from heat. Season with pepper. Garnish with celery leaves and chives.

➤ **MAKE AHEAD:** Prepare through Step 3 and refrigerate stew and oysters separately for up to 1 day. To serve, reheat and finish with Step 4.

SERVES 12: ABOUT ¾ CUP EACH

Calories 147 | Fat 8g (sat 5g) | Cholesterol 41mg | Carbs 11g | Total sugars 5g (added 0g) | Protein 7g | Fiber 1g | Sodium 299mg | Potassium 283mg.
Nutrition bonus: Vitamin B_{12} (210% daily value) | Iron (25% dv).

Don't worry about shucking the oysters. Most supermarket seafood departments carry them already shucked.

CHILLED STRAWBERRY-RHUBARB SOUP

Sweet strawberries and tart rhubarb are whirled together in this chilled soup. Serve it as a starter for an early-summer supper.

 4 cups ½-inch pieces rhubarb, fresh *or* frozen

 3 cups water

1½ cups sliced strawberries

 ¼ cup sugar

 ⅛ teaspoon salt

 ⅓ cup chopped fresh basil *or* mint, plus more
    for garnish

   Ground pepper to taste

1. Bring rhubarb and water to a boil in a large saucepan. Cook until the rhubarb is very soft and broken down, about 5 minutes. Transfer to a medium bowl. Put a couple inches of ice water in a large bowl and set the bowl with the rhubarb in it to help cool it quickly. (If you aren't in a hurry, you can skip the ice-water bath.) Refrigerate, stirring occasionally, until cool, at least 20 minutes.

2. Transfer the rhubarb to a blender. Add strawberries, sugar and salt; blend until smooth. Return to the bowl and stir in basil (or mint). Serve sprinkled with more herbs and a generous grinding of pepper.

➤ **MAKE AHEAD:** Refrigerate the soup (without basil or mint) for up to 1 day. Stir in herbs just before serving.

SERVES 4: ABOUT 1¼ CUPS EACH

Calories 95 | Fat 0g (sat 0g) | Cholesterol 0mg | Carbs 23g | Total sugars 17g (added 13g) | Protein 2g | Fiber 4g | Sodium 84mg | Potassium 460mg.
Nutrition bonus: Vitamin C (78% daily value).

CELERIAC AND APPLE SOUP WITH BLUE CHEESE TOASTS

Roasting celeriac and apples before pureeing them into the soup intensifies their flavor. The blue cheese toasts add a little something special, but you could garnish with toasted pecans instead.

SOUP

- 2 pounds celeriac (celery root)
- 2 medium Granny Smith apples, peeled
- 3 tablespoons extra-virgin olive oil, divided
- ¾ teaspoon salt, divided
- 1 medium onion, chopped
- 1 large carrot, chopped
- 2 teaspoons chopped fresh thyme
- 2 teaspoons finely chopped garlic
- 1 medium russet potato (about 8 ounces), peeled and chopped
- 4 cups low-sodium vegetable broth
- 2 cups water
- ¼ teaspoon freshly grated nutmeg
- ¼ teaspoon ground pepper

TOASTS

- 8 slices baguette (¼-inch), preferably whole-wheat
- 1 clove garlic, peeled and halved
- 8 teaspoons crumbled Gorgonzola *or* other mild blue cheese

1. To prepare soup: Position rack in center of oven; preheat to 450°F.

2. Cut one end off celeriac to create a flat surface to keep it steady, then cut off the skin, following the contour of the root. (Or use a vegetable peeler and peel around the root at least three times to ensure all the fibrous skin has been removed.) Cut into ½-inch pieces. Cut apples into 1-inch wedges. Toss the celeriac and apples in a large bowl with 2 tablespoons oil and ¼ teaspoon salt until well coated. Spread out on a baking sheet. Roast, stirring once or twice, until lightly browned and tender, 35 to 40 minutes.

3. Meanwhile, heat the remaining 1 tablespoon oil in a large pot over medium heat. Add onion, carrot and thyme; cook, stirring, until softened but not browned, about 5 minutes. Add chopped garlic and cook, stirring, for 30 seconds. Add potato, broth, water, nutmeg, pepper and the remaining ½ teaspoon salt. Bring to a boil. Reduce heat to maintain a gentle simmer, cover and cook until the vegetables smash easily when pressed against the side of the pot, 35 to 40 minutes. Add the celeriac mixture to the pot. Puree the soup with an immersion blender until smooth. (Or transfer the soup to a blender and blend until smooth. Use caution when pureeing hot liquids.)

4. To prepare toasts: About 15 minutes before you're ready to serve, preheat oven to 400°F.

5. Place baguette slices on a baking sheet and bake until toasted, 6 to 8 minutes. Rub them with garlic, then top with cheese. Return to the oven and bake until the cheese is melted, 5 to 7 minutes.

6. Serve the soup topped with a cheese toast.

▶▶ **MAKE AHEAD:** Prepare soup (Steps 1–3) and refrigerate for up to 3 days. Reheat over medium-low and prepare cheese toasts 15 minutes before serving.

SERVES 8: ABOUT 1 CUP SOUP & 1 CHEESE TOAST EACH

Calories 174 | Fat 7g (sat 1g) | **Cholesterol** 2mg | **Carbs** 26g | Total sugars 8g (added 0g) | **Protein** 3g | **Fiber** 4g | Sodium 446mg | **Potassium** 487mg.
Nutrition bonus: Vitamin A (32% daily value).

CREAMY RYE AND BUTTERNUT SQUASH SOUP

This is a healthier take on a traditional squash and rye bread soup from the Valle d'Aosta region of Italy, usually made with milk and cheese. This variation gets its richness from the creamy starches released by the bread and winter squash. If you like caraway, be sure to use a seeded rye bread.

2 tablespoons extra-virgin olive oil

2 cloves garlic, minced

¼ teaspoon crushed red pepper

4½ cups diced butternut, kabocha *or* hubbard squash (1-inch pieces)

6 cups water

¾ teaspoon kosher *or* sea salt

5 cups 1-inch pieces stale rye bread without crust (*see Tip*)

2 tablespoons finely chopped fresh parsley

1. Heat oil in a large pot over medium heat. Add garlic and crushed red pepper; cook, stirring, until fragrant, about 1 minute. Add squash and stir to coat with the oil. Add water and salt. Bring to a boil. Reduce heat to a simmer and cook, partially covered, until the squash is tender, 15 to 20 minutes.

2. Mash about half the squash against the side of the pot to create a thick broth. Stir in bread; return to a simmer and cook, stirring occasionally, until the bread is beginning to break apart, 5 to 15 minutes (cooking time depends on how stale and/or dense your bread is).

3. Remove the soup from the heat, cover and let stand for 15 minutes. Stir in parsley and serve.

SERVES 6: 1⅓ CUPS EACH

Calories 185 | Fat 6g (sat 1g) | Cholesterol 0mg | Carbs 30g | Total sugars 4g (added 1g) | Protein 4g | Fiber 4g | Sodium 480mg | Potassium 413mg.
Nutrition bonus: Vitamin A (205% daily value) | Vitamin C (37% dv).

To stale bread naturally, store at room temperature in a paper (not plastic) bag for 2 to 5 days. If you don't want to wait, bake sliced or cubed bread on a large baking sheet at 250°F until crisped and dry, 15 to 20 minutes. One 1-pound loaf (12 to 14 slices) yields 8 to 10 cups 1-inch pieces.

JERUSALEM ARTICHOKE–POTATO SOUP WITH CRISPY CROUTONS

Jerusalem artichokes—also known as sunchokes—are the knobby tuber roots of sunflowers. They have a delicate chestnut-like flavor and a starchy texture, making them a perfect partner for potatoes in this soup. Serve as a starter before a fall or winter dinner alongside a hearty green salad.

- 3 tablespoons extra-virgin olive oil, divided
- 1 large leek *or* 2 small leeks, cleaned and thinly sliced *(see Tip, page 197)*
- 3 cloves garlic, minced
- 5 cups low-sodium chicken broth *or* vegetable broth
- 1 pound Jerusalem artichokes, peeled and chopped
- 8 ounces Yukon Gold potatoes, peeled and diced
- ¾ teaspoon salt
- ½ cup half-and-half
- 2 teaspoons fresh thyme leaves, plus more for garnish
- 3 cups cubed whole-wheat bread
- ½ teaspoon garlic powder
- ½ teaspoon ground pepper

1. Heat 1 tablespoon oil in a large pot over medium heat. Add leek and cook, stirring, until softened, about 5 minutes. Stir in garlic. Cook 1 minute more. Add broth, Jerusalem artichokes, potatoes and salt; bring to a boil. Reduce heat and simmer, covered, until the vegetables are very tender, 20 to 25 minutes.

2. Puree the soup with an immersion blender until smooth. (Or transfer the soup to a blender and blend until smooth. Use caution when blending hot liquids.) Stir in half-and-half and thyme.

3. Meanwhile, preheat oven to 425°F. Place bread cubes on a baking sheet. Drizzle with the remaining 2 tablespoons oil, then sprinkle with garlic powder and pepper; toss to coat. Bake, stirring once halfway through, until browned and crisp, 15 to 20 minutes.

4. Serve the soup topped with the croutons and more thyme, if desired.

SERVES 8: ABOUT 1 CUP EACH

Calories 199 | Fat 8g (sat 2g) | Cholesterol 5mg | Carbs 25g | Total sugars 6g (added 1g) | Protein 7g | Fiber 3g | Sodium 364mg | Potassium 482mg.

SHRIMP *AND* CHINESE CHIVE WONTON SOUP

Chinese chives taste like a cross between a leek and a ramp with a garlicky edge. Trim the stem end before using. Look for them at farmers' markets and at Asian markets or use regular chives.

2 **Chinese dried mushrooms** *or* **dried shiitakes**

4½ **cups low-sodium chicken broth, divided**

4 **ounces raw medium shrimp, peeled and deveined**

¼ **cup minced chives, preferably Chinese chives**

2 **tablespoons minced water chestnuts**

2 **teaspoons Shao Hsing rice wine** *or* **dry sherry**

7 **teaspoons toasted sesame oil, divided**

¼ **teaspoon ground white pepper**

1 **tablespoon cornstarch**

24 **square fresh wonton wrappers**

4 **¼-inch slices fresh ginger, peeled and smashed**

12 **yau choi (choi sum)** *or* **broccolini stalks**

2½ **tablespoons reduced-sodium soy sauce**

Cilantro sprigs (optional)

1. Place mushrooms in a small heatproof bowl. Heat ½ cup broth until steaming and pour over the mushrooms. Let stand until softened, about 30 minutes. Remove the mushrooms (reserve the liquid); discard the stems and finely chop the caps.

2. Cut shrimp into ¼-inch pieces. Combine the shrimp, the mushrooms, chives, water chestnuts, rice wine (or sherry), 1 teaspoon sesame oil and pepper in a bowl.

3. Line a baking sheet with parchment and dust with cornstarch. Loosely cover wonton wrappers with a barely damp kitchen towel. Take 6 of the wrappers and set in a row with one corner toward you. Place a rounded teaspoon of the shrimp filling on the bottom corner of each wrapper. Starting at the bottom, roll each wrapper up three-quarters of the way, tucking in the filling as you go. Press on both sides to seal. Lightly dab a few drops of water on one of two side corners, bring the side corners together, overlap them and press to seal. Place the filled wontons on the prepared pan. Repeat in 3 more batches to make 24 wontons.

4. Put 2 quarts of water on to boil in a large pot for cooking the wontons.

5. Meanwhile, combine the remaining 4 cups broth, the reserved mushroom-soaking liquid and ginger in a large saucepan; cover and bring to a boil. Add yau choi (or broccolini) and cook until tender-crisp, 1 to 2 minutes. Remove from heat. Discard ginger. Divide the greens among 6 soup bowls and drizzle with 1 teaspoon sesame oil each. Stir soy sauce into the broth; cover to keep warm.

6. Add half the wontons to the boiling water and return to a boil over high heat, nudging them with a slotted spoon to prevent them from sticking. Reduce heat to medium and gently simmer until all the wontons float to the surface, 2 to 4 minutes. Use the slotted spoon to divide the wontons among 3 of the bowls, then ladle about ¾ cup broth over each portion. Repeat with the remaining wontons and broth. Serve hot, garnished with cilantro, if desired.

SERVES 6: 2 STALKS OF GREENS, 4 WONTONS & ¾ CUP BROTH EACH

Calories 202 | Fat 7g (sat 1g) | Cholesterol 26mg | Carbs 24g | Total sugars 1g (added 0g) | Protein 11g | Fiber 1g | Sodium 485mg | Potassium 271mg.
Nutrition bonus: Vitamin C (46% daily value) | Vitamin A (39% dv).

WILD MUSHROOM SOUP

This creamy mushroom soup recipe showcases the savory flavor of fresh morel mushrooms. If you can't find fresh or dried morels, try other dried mushrooms, such as dried shiitakes or creminis, but be sure to use at least 1 ounce dried mushrooms to keep the luscious flavor. Serve with crusty garlic bread.

12 ounces fresh morels, trimmed, *or* 1 ounce dried morels plus 12 ounces fresh cremini (baby bella) mushrooms

5 cups low-sodium chicken *or* vegetable broth, or as needed

2 tablespoons extra-virgin olive oil, plus more for garnish

1 medium carrot, finely chopped

1 stalk celery, finely chopped

1 small onion, finely chopped

1 tablespoon finely chopped garlic

¼ cup Marsala *or* dry sherry

1 cup diced peeled potato

1½ teaspoons finely chopped fresh thyme

1½ teaspoons kosher salt

⅛ teaspoon crushed red pepper, or to taste
  Ground pepper to taste

¼ cup coarsely chopped flat-leaf parsley

1. If using fresh morels, cut in half and briefly swish in a large bowl of tepid water. Drain and repeat to remove all the dirt. Gently but thoroughly pat dry, then coarsely chop. (If using dried morels, soak in 2 cups warm water for 30 minutes. Strain in a cheesecloth-lined sieve and reserve the soaking liquid. Add enough broth to the soaking liquid to equal 5 cups. Coarsely chop the morels and creminis.)

2. Heat oil in a large pot over medium heat. Add carrot, celery and onion; cover and cook, stirring occasionally, until the vegetables are tender, 8 to 10 minutes. Add garlic and cook, stirring frequently, for 30 seconds. Add Marsala (or sherry) and cook for 1 minute more.

3. Add the broth, the fresh mushrooms (and dried, if using), potato, thyme, salt and crushed red pepper. Bring to a boil. Reduce heat and simmer, uncovered, until the potato is tender, 15 to 20 minutes.

4. Puree the soup with an immersion blender or in a regular blender or food processor. (Use caution when blending hot liquids.) Season with pepper. Serve the soup topped with parsley and a drizzle of oil, if desired.

➤ **MAKE AHEAD:** Refrigerate for up to 3 days.

SERVES 8: ¾ CUP EACH

Calories 108 | Fat 5g (sat 1g) | Cholesterol 0mg | Carbs 11g | Total sugars 2g (added 0g) | Protein 5g | Fiber 2g | Sodium 426mg | Potassium 443mg.
Nutrition bonus: Iron (32% daily value) | Vitamin A (29% dv).

EAT MORE VEG!

You thought salad was the best way to get vegetables? Think again. A bowl of brothy goodness can accommodate a great variety of veggies. And while all our soups put an emphasis on fresh produce, the ones in this chapter offer up an even bigger bounty of veggies in an array of tasty forms—creamy and chunky, hot or chilled.

GRILLED TOMATO
GAZPACHO
PAGE 32

GRILLED TOMATO GAZPACHO

Grill the vegetables for this refreshing soup earlier in the day or even the night before. *(Photo: page 30.)*

2 pounds ripe plum tomatoes

1 small red bell pepper

1 English cucumber, peeled and seeded, divided

½ cup torn fresh *or* day-old country bread (crusts removed)

1 small clove garlic

2-3 tablespoons red-wine vinegar

1 tablespoon chopped fresh parsley

¼ teaspoon piment d'Espelette (*see Tip*) *or* hot Spanish paprika *or* pinch of cayenne pepper

½ teaspoon salt

¼ teaspoon ground pepper

2 tablespoons extra-virgin olive oil

1. Preheat grill to medium-high.

2. Grill tomatoes and bell pepper, turning a few times, until they soften and the skins are blistered and charred in spots, about 8 minutes. Transfer the pepper to a plastic bag and let it steam until cool enough to handle. Peel off the skin; cut the pepper in half and discard the stem and seeds. Place one half in a blender. When the tomatoes are cool enough to handle, core and roughly chop. Add the tomatoes, skins and all, to the blender.

3. Add half the cucumber to the blender along with bread, garlic, vinegar to taste, parsley, piment d'Espelette (or paprika or cayenne), salt and pepper. Blend until smooth. Add oil and blend until well combined. Refrigerate until room temperature or chilled, at least 1 hour.

4. Before serving, finely dice the remaining cucumber and bell pepper. Stir half of each into the gazpacho and use the rest for garnish.

▸▸ **MAKE AHEAD:** Prepare through Step 3 and refrigerate for up to 1 day. Stir to recombine and garnish just before serving.

SERVES 6: 1 SCANT CUP EACH

Calories 84 | Fat 5g (sat 1g) | Cholesterol 0mg | Carbs 9g | Total sugars 5g (added 0g) | Protein 2g | Fiber 2g | Sodium 219mg | Potassium 405mg.
Nutrition bonus: Vitamin C (61% daily value) | Vitamin A (32% dv).

Piment d'Espelette is a sweet, mildly spicy pepper from the French side of the Basque region, ground into powder.

PAPRIKA *and* RED PEPPER SOUP WITH PISTACHIOS

Richly satisfying, this luscious soup combines capsaicin from both paprika and its hot-blooded sibling, Thai chile. Gifts from Spain, Hungary and South America, paprika and chiles infuse the soup with robust color and gentle heat. For an extra-nutty flavor, puree an additional ¼ cup shelled pistachios with ¼ cup water and serve the soup with a dollop of pistachio puree on top.

2 tablespoons canola oil

1 small onion, diced

2 large red bell peppers, seeded and diced

1-2 fresh green Thai *or* serrano chiles, stemmed and coarsely chopped

2 teaspoons sweet Hungarian paprika

¾ teaspoon kosher *or* sea salt

½ teaspoon ground cardamom

½ cup unsalted shelled pistachios

2 cups low-sodium vegetable broth *or* water

1 cup buttermilk

2 tablespoons whipping cream

¼ cup finely chopped fresh cilantro *or* basil

1. Heat oil in a large saucepan over medium-high heat. Add onion, bell peppers and chiles to taste. Cook, stirring, until the vegetables release some of their juices and the onion is lightly browned, 3 to 5 minutes. Sprinkle the vegetables with paprika, salt and cardamom and cook, stirring, until the spices are very fragrant, 1 to 2 minutes.

2. Stir in pistachios and broth (or water). Bring to a boil. Reduce the heat to medium-low and simmer, covered, stirring occasionally, until the peppers are fork-tender, 20 to 25 minutes. Remove from the heat; let cool 5 minutes.

3. Transfer the soup to a blender (in batches if necessary) and puree until smooth. (Use caution when blending hot liquids.) Return the soup to the pan.

4. Whisk buttermilk and cream in a bowl; stir into the soup. Gently warm over low heat. Serve sprinkled with cilantro (or basil).

▸▸ **MAKE AHEAD:** Refrigerate for up to 2 days.

SERVES 4: ABOUT 1 CUP EACH

Calories 242 | Fat 17g (sat 3g) | Cholesterol 9mg | Carbs 17g | Total sugars 10g (added 0g) | Protein 7g | Fiber 5g | Sodium 493mg | Potassium 415mg.
Nutrition bonus: Vitamin C (179% daily value) | Vitamin A (67% dv).

TOMATO SOUP

This simple tomato soup is perfect paired with your favorite grilled cheese sandwich.
Make a double batch and freeze the extra for rainy-day emergencies.

1 **tablespoon extra-virgin olive oil**

1 **tablespoon butter**

1 **medium onion, chopped**

1 **stalk celery, chopped**

2 **cloves garlic, chopped**

1 **teaspoon chopped fresh thyme** *or* **parsley**

1 **28-ounce can whole peeled tomatoes**

1 **14-ounce can whole peeled tomatoes**

4 **cups reduced-sodium chicken broth,
    "no-chicken" broth** *(see page 224) or*
    vegetable broth

½ **cup half-and-half (optional)**

½ **teaspoon salt**

 Ground pepper to taste

1. Heat oil and butter in a large pot over medium heat until the butter melts. Add onion and celery and cook, stirring occasionally, until softened, 4 to 6 minutes. Add garlic and thyme (or parsley); cook, stirring, until fragrant, about 10 seconds.

2. Stir in canned tomatoes with their juices. Add broth and bring to a lively simmer over high heat. Reduce heat to maintain a lively simmer and cook for 10 minutes.

3. Puree the soup in the pot using an immersion blender or in batches in a blender. (Use caution when blending hot liquids.) Stir in half-and-half (if using), salt and pepper.

▸▸ **MAKE AHEAD:** Refrigerate for up to 4 days or freeze for up to 3 months.

SERVES 8: ABOUT 1 CUP EACH

Calories 79 | Fat 4g (sat 1g) | Cholesterol 4mg | Carbs 8g |
Total sugars 4g (added 0g) | Protein 4g | Fiber 3g |
Sodium 357mg | Potassium 426mg.
Nutrition bonus: Vitamin C (34% daily value).

ITALIAN BREAD *AND* TOMATO SOUP

Inspired by Tuscany's legendary *pappa al pomodoro*, this soup is a great way to use up stale bread. The traditional version doesn't contain kale or a topping of squash and grape tomatoes, but why not?

¾ cup diced summer squash

½ cup quartered grape tomatoes

2 tablespoons lemon juice

4 tablespoons extra-virgin olive oil, divided

Pinch of sugar

Pinch of salt

Pinch of crushed red pepper

4 cups torn *or* cubed stale country bread, crusts removed

1 cup chopped onion

½ cup chopped carrot

3 cloves garlic, minced

1 teaspoon fennel seed, crushed

3 pounds very ripe tomatoes, peeled (*see* **Tip**), seeded and chopped, *or* one 28-ounce can plus one 15-ounce can San Marzano diced tomatoes

4 cups low-sodium chicken broth

1½ cups chopped kale

½ cup chopped fresh basil, plus more for garnish

¼ teaspoon ground pepper

1. Combine squash, grape tomatoes, lemon juice, 1 tablespoon oil, sugar, salt and crushed red pepper in a medium bowl. Set aside.

2. Heat 2 tablespoons oil in a large pot over medium heat. Add bread and cook, stirring, until starting to brown, about 4 minutes. Transfer to a bowl, scraping the pan clean with a spatula.

3. Add the remaining 1 tablespoon oil, onion, carrot, garlic and fennel seed to the pot. Cook on medium-low, stirring occasionally, until tender but not brown, 3 to 5 minutes. Add tomatoes and all their juices, broth and the bread. Bring to a boil. Reduce heat to a simmer and cook, uncovered, for 20 minutes.

4. Add kale, basil and pepper. Simmer for 10 minutes more. Serve the soup topped with the squash mixture and garnished with more basil, if desired.

SERVES 6: 1½ CUPS EACH

Calories 269 | Fat 11g (sat 2g) | Cholesterol 0mg | Carbs 36g | Total sugars 8g (added 0g) | Protein 9g | Fiber 5g | Sodium 234mg | Potassium 785mg.
Nutrition bonus: Vitamin A (84% daily value) | Vitamin C (71% dv).

To peel tomatoes, cut a small X in the bottom and plunge into boiling water until the skins are slightly loosened, 30 seconds to 2 minutes. Transfer to a bowl of ice water for 1 minute. Peel with a paring knife, starting at the X.

SMOKED GOUDA-BROCCOLI SOUP

Smoked paprika and smoked Gouda give this soup a double hit of smoky flavor. Smoked paprika comes in both sweet and hot varieties—the sweeter one is more commonly available.

1½ **pounds broccoli crowns (2 medium)**
2 **tablespoons extra-virgin olive oil, divided**
1 **cup chopped sweet onion**
2 **cloves garlic, smashed and peeled**
1 **tablespoon all-purpose flour**
⅛ **teaspoon smoked paprika**
4 **cups low-sodium chicken broth**
2 **cups cubed rye bread (½-inch pieces)**
1 **cup shredded smoked Gouda cheese**
2 **teaspoons white-wine vinegar**
½ **teaspoon salt**
½ **teaspoon ground white pepper**

1. Cut 1½ cups bite-size broccoli florets and set aside. Coarsely chop the remaining broccoli.

2. Heat 1 tablespoon oil in a large saucepan over medium heat. Add onion and cook, stirring occasionally, until soft, about 5 minutes. Add garlic and cook, stirring, for 30 seconds. Add flour and paprika; stir to coat. Add broth and the chopped broccoli. Bring to a boil over high heat. Reduce to a gentle simmer and cook, stirring occasionally, until the broccoli is tender, 8 to 10 minutes.

3. Meanwhile, make croutons: Toss bread with the remaining 1 tablespoon oil in a large skillet. Cook over medium heat, stirring occasionally, until browned and crisp, about 10 minutes. Transfer to a bowl.

4. Puree the soup in a blender, in batches if necessary, or use an immersion blender. (Use caution when blending hot liquids.) Return the soup to the pan over low heat. Add cheese a little at a time, stirring constantly until it melts before adding more. Stir in the reserved broccoli florets. Cook, stirring occasionally, until they are bright green, 2 to 3 minutes. Stir in vinegar, salt and white pepper. Serve hot, topped with the croutons.

SERVES 4: 1½ CUPS SOUP & ¼ CUP CROUTONS EACH

Calories 316 | Fat 16g (sat 5g) | Cholesterol 24mg | Carbs 31g | Total sugars 6g (added 0g) | Protein 17g | Fiber 7g | Sodium 723mg | Potassium 873mg.
Nutrition bonus: Vitamin C (259% daily value) | Folate (37% dv) | Calcium (27% dv) | Vitamin A (24% dv).

If you can't find smoked Gouda, smoked Cheddar gives delicious results as well.

SPICY BUTTERNUT SQUASH SOUP

This silky-smooth soup has Southwestern flair and gets a kick of spice from cumin, chipotle and cloves. Other winter squash, such as buttercup, acorn, kabocha and kuri, are also delicious in it. *(Photo: page 2.)*

1½ **pounds butternut *or* other winter squash**

1 **tablespoon canola oil**

2 **stalks celery, chopped**

1 **small onion, diced**

1 **carrot, chopped**

1 **teaspoon ground cumin**

¼-½ **teaspoon ground chipotle chile**

⅛ **teaspoon ground cloves**

6 **cups low-sodium vegetable broth**

1 **teaspoon sea salt**

¼ **teaspoon ground pepper**

½ **cup low-fat plain yogurt**

2 **tablespoons snipped fresh chives *or* chopped parsley**

1. Preheat oven to 350°F.

2. Cut squash in half and seed. Place the halves on a baking sheet, cut-side down. Bake until tender when pierced with a knife, 45 minutes to 1 hour. Scoop out flesh when cool enough to handle.

3. Heat oil in a large saucepan over medium heat. Add celery, onion and carrot and stir to coat. Cover, reduce heat to medium-low and cook, stirring frequently, until soft, 8 to 10 minutes. Stir in the squash flesh, cumin, chipotle to taste and cloves. Add broth and simmer, covered, until the vegetables are very tender, 20 to 25 minutes.

4. Puree the soup with an immersion blender or in a blender (in batches) until smooth. (Use caution when blending hot liquids.) Season with salt and pepper. Garnish with yogurt and chives (or parsley).

SERVES 6: ABOUT 1¼ CUPS EACH

Calories 104 | Fat 3g (sat 0g) | Cholesterol 1mg | Carbs 18g | Total sugars 7g (added 0g) | Protein 2g | Fiber 4g | Sodium 544mg | Potassium 473mg.
Nutrition bonus: Vitamin A (239% daily value) | Vitamin C (38% dv).

LOW-CALORIE • VEGETARIAN • GLUTEN-FREE

ACTIVE 15 MIN
TOTAL 1½ HRS

AMAZING PEA SOUP

Sometimes the peas in the garden outpace the picking or the supplies in the store aren't so fabulous. Here's a recipe for those less-than-perfect peas that uses the whole pea, shell and all, so there's no shucking involved. A soup for the true pea lover.

12 cups water
2 pounds English peas, unshelled
⅓ cup finely chopped fresh dill, plus sprigs for garnish
1 teaspoon salt
Ground pepper to taste
¾ cup low-fat plain yogurt

1. Bring water to a boil in a large pot. Add peas, return to a boil and then reduce to a simmer. Cook, stirring occasionally, for 45 minutes.

2. Using a slotted spoon, transfer one-third of the pea pods to a food processor. Add ½ cup cooking liquid and process until smooth. (Use caution when blending hot liquids.) Pour into a large bowl. Repeat with the remaining pea pods in 2 batches, with ½ cup cooking liquid each time. Pour the pureed peas plus the remaining cooking liquid through a fine-mesh sieve, pressing on the solids to extract as much liquid as possible. *(Alternatively, put through a food mill fitted with a fine disc.)*

3. Return the soup to the pot, bring to a boil and then simmer until reduced by about a third (to about 6 cups), 30 to 35 minutes. Stir in dill, salt and pepper. Ladle into bowls and top each serving with a swirl or dollop of yogurt and a sprig of dill, if desired.

SERVES 6: ABOUT 1 CUP EACH

Calories 79 | Fat 1g (sat 0g) | Cholesterol 2mg | Carbs 13g | Total sugars 8g (added 0g) | Protein 6g | Fiber 4g | Sodium 429mg | Potassium 365mg.
Nutrition bonus: Vitamin C (143% daily value) | Vitamin A (32% dv).

Peas begin to lose their sugar content the minute they're picked, so the sooner they get from the garden to the cooking pot, the better.

CALDO TLALPEÑO (MEXICAN CHICKEN SOUP)

Epazote [eh-pah-ZOH-teh] is an aromatic herb that is used almost exclusively in Mexican and Guatemalan cooking. It has a pungent, slightly medicinal flavor with notes of oregano, anise, citrus and mint. It's not crucial in this soup, but it is interesting. Its singular flavor makes it not worth replacing if you can't find it—but if you can, by all means give it a try!

3 pounds bone-in, skin-on chicken drumsticks and thighs

¼ medium white onion plus 1 diced medium white onion, divided

10 cups water, divided, plus more as needed

3½ teaspoons kosher salt, divided

2 ears corn, husked

1 pound russet potatoes, cut into 1-inch pieces

2 medium carrots, cut into 1-inch pieces

2 medium chayote squash or yellow summer squash, cut into 1-inch pieces

2 cups green beans (1½-inch pieces)

1 medium zucchini, halved lengthwise and sliced into ½-inch pieces

1 tablespoon corn oil

2 large plum tomatoes, diced

8 cremini (baby bella) mushrooms, sliced

2 tablespoons chopped chipotle chiles in adobo sauce

15 fresh epazote leaves, chopped (optional)

1. Place chicken and ¼ onion in a large pot. Add 8 cups water and 1½ teaspoons salt. Bring to a boil and skim off any foam from the surface. Reduce heat to a gentle simmer, cover and cook until the chicken is just cooked through but not yet pulling away from the bone, about 20 minutes. Remove the chicken to a bowl; discard the onion. Reserve the broth.

2. Meanwhile, place corn, potatoes, carrots and squash in a 10- to 12-quart stockpot.

3. Set aside ¼ cup broth. Add enough water to the remaining broth to equal 10 cups and add to the stockpot with the vegetables. Add the remaining 2 teaspoons salt. Cover and bring to a boil over high heat. Add green beans. Reduce heat to maintain a simmer; cover and cook until the vegetables are slightly tender but not completely cooked, 8 to 10 minutes. Add zucchini. Remove from heat and add the chicken; cover to keep warm.

4. Heat oil in a large skillet over medium heat. Add diced onion and cook, stirring often, until translucent, 4 to 6 minutes. Add tomatoes and cook until softened, about 3 minutes. Stir in mushrooms and the reserved ¼ cup broth; bring to a simmer. Reduce heat to medium-low, cover and cook, stirring occasionally, until the mushrooms are tender, about 10 minutes. Stir in chipotles. Transfer the mixture to the stockpot and stir to combine. Add epazote leaves (if using). Cover and cook the soup over medium-low heat until the vegetables are tender, about 10 minutes more. Serve the soup in large deep bowls.

▸▸ **MAKE AHEAD:** Refrigerate for up to 3 days.

SERVES 10: 2⅓ CUPS EACH

Calories 258 | Fat 11g (sat 3g) | Cholesterol 60mg | Carbs 20g | Total sugars 5g (added 0g) | Protein 21g | Fiber 3g | Sodium 766mg | Potassium 685mg. Nutrition bonus: Vitamin A (49% daily value) | Vitamin C (28% dv) | Folate (20% dv).

ACTIVE   40 MIN
TOTAL   1 HR

MEXICAN CABBAGE SOUP

Although it's abundant in this hearty soup, cabbage isn't the only vegetable contributing texture and nutrition. Carrot, celery, peppers—and a topping of healthy-fat-packed avocado—make this pleasantly spicy soup good all around.

2 tablespoons extra-virgin olive oil

2 cups chopped onions

1 cup chopped carrot

1 cup chopped celery

1 cup chopped poblano *or* green bell pepper

4 large cloves garlic, minced

8 cups sliced cabbage

1 tablespoon tomato paste

1 tablespoon minced chipotle chile in adobo sauce (*see Tip*)

1 teaspoon ground cumin

½ teaspoon ground coriander

4 cups low-sodium vegetable broth *or* chicken broth

4 cups water

2 15-ounce cans pinto *or* black beans, rinsed

¾ teaspoon salt

½ cup chopped fresh cilantro, plus more for serving

2 tablespoons lime juice

Crumbled queso fresco, nonfat plain Greek yogurt *and/or* diced avocado for garnish

1. Heat oil in a large soup pot (8-quart or larger) over medium heat. Add onions, carrot, celery, poblano (or bell pepper) and garlic; cook, stirring frequently, until softened, 10 to 12 minutes. Add cabbage; cook, stirring occasionally, until slightly softened, about 10 minutes more. Add tomato paste, chipotle, cumin and coriander; cook, stirring, for 1 minute more.

2. Add broth, water, beans and salt. Cover and bring to a boil over high heat. Reduce heat and simmer, partially covered, until the vegetables are tender, about 10 minutes. Remove from heat and stir in cilantro and lime juice. Serve garnished with cheese, yogurt and/or avocado, if desired.

SERVES 8: ABOUT 1½ CUPS EACH

Calories 167 | Fat 4g (sat 1g) | Cholesterol 0mg | Carbs 27g | Total sugars 7g (added 0g) | Protein 7g | Fiber 9g | Sodium 408mg | Potassium 624mg.
Nutrition bonus: Vitamin C (79% daily value) | Vitamin A (59% dv).

Leftover chipotle chiles in adobo sauce freeze well. Divide into 1- to 2-tablespoon portions before freezing in small freezer bags or ice cube trays.

SMOKY CHICKEN-CHILE SOUP WITH TAMALE DUMPLINGS

These pillowy, tamale-like dumplings made with masa harina are toothsome bites of cheesy, corny goodness.

DUMPLINGS

- 1 cup masa harina
- ½ cup low-sodium chicken broth
- ¼ cup shredded Monterey Jack cheese
- 2 tablespoons extra-virgin olive oil
- ¼ teaspoon ground cumin *or* chili powder
- ¼ teaspoon salt

SOUP

- 1 tablespoon extra-virgin olive oil
- 1 cup chopped onion
- 1½ teaspoons ground cumin *or* chili powder
- 3½ cups low-sodium chicken broth
- 2 15-ounce cans fire-roasted diced tomatoes
- 4 cups shredded cooked chicken
- 2 cups frozen corn
- 1-2 tablespoons chopped chipotle chiles in adobo sauce
- 1 cup quartered and sliced zucchini
- 2 tablespoons lime juice

Chopped cilantro & lime wedges for garnish

1. To prepare dumplings: Combine masa harina, ½ cup broth, cheese, 2 tablespoons oil, ¼ teaspoon cumin (or chili powder) and salt in a medium bowl. Roll the dough into 18 round dumplings, using a scant 1 tablespoon for each.

2. To prepare soup: Heat oil in a large pot over medium-high heat. Add onion and cumin (or chili powder) and cook, stirring, until soft, about 4 minutes. Stir in broth, tomatoes with their juices, chicken, corn and chipotles to taste. Bring to a boil over high heat.

3. Add the dumplings and zucchini. Reduce heat to medium, cover and cook until the dumplings and zucchini are tender, 5 to 7 minutes. Add lime juice. Serve the soup topped with cilantro, with lime wedges on the side, if desired.

▸▸ **MAKE AHEAD:** Prepare dumplings (Step 1) and refrigerate for up to 1 day.

SERVES 6: 1¾ CUPS EACH

Calories 429 | Fat 19g (sat 5g) | Cholesterol 128mg | Carbs 37g | Total sugars 7g (added 0g) | Protein 33g | Fiber 5g | Sodium 664mg | Potassium 650mg. Nutrition bonus: Vitamin C (69% daily value).

ROASTED CAULIFLOWER *AND* POTATO CURRY SOUP

Roasting the cauliflower first adds depth and prevents the florets from turning to mush. A little tomato sauce and coconut milk give the broth a silky texture. Serve with a dollop of sour cream or yogurt, if desired.

2 teaspoons ground coriander

2 teaspoons ground cumin

1½ teaspoons ground cinnamon

1½ teaspoons ground turmeric

1¼ teaspoons salt

¾ teaspoon ground pepper

⅛ teaspoon cayenne pepper

1 small head cauliflower, cut into small florets (about 6 cups)

2 tablespoons extra-virgin olive oil, divided

1 large onion, chopped

1 cup diced carrot

3 large cloves garlic, minced

1½ teaspoons grated fresh ginger

1 fresh red chile pepper, such as serrano *or* jalapeño, minced, plus more for garnish

1 14-ounce can no-salt-added tomato sauce

4 cups low-sodium vegetable broth

3 cups diced peeled russet potatoes (½-inch)

3 cups diced peeled sweet potatoes (½-inch)

2 teaspoons lime zest

2 tablespoons lime juice

1 14-ounce can coconut milk

Chopped fresh cilantro for garnish

1. Preheat oven to 450°F.

2. Combine coriander, cumin, cinnamon, turmeric, salt, pepper and cayenne in a small bowl. Toss cauliflower with 1 tablespoon oil in a large bowl, sprinkle with 1 tablespoon of the spice mixture and toss again. Spread in a single layer on a rimmed baking sheet. Roast the cauliflower until the edges are browned, 15 to 20 minutes. Set aside.

3. Meanwhile, heat the remaining 1 tablespoon oil in a large pot over medium-high heat. Add onion and carrot and cook, stirring often, until starting to brown, 3 to 4 minutes. Reduce heat to medium and continue cooking, stirring often, until the onion is soft, 3 to 4 minutes. Add garlic, ginger, chile and the remaining spice mixture. Cook, stirring, for 1 minute more.

4. Stir in tomato sauce, scraping up any browned bits, and simmer for 1 minute. Add broth, potatoes, sweet potatoes, lime zest and juice. Cover and bring to a boil over high heat. Reduce heat to maintain a gentle simmer and cook, partially covered and stirring occasionally, until the vegetables are tender, 35 to 40 minutes.

5. Stir in coconut milk and the roasted cauliflower. Return to a simmer to heat through. Serve garnished with cilantro and chiles, if desired.

➤➤ **MAKE AHEAD:** Refrigerate for up to 5 days.

SERVES 8: ABOUT 1½ CUPS EACH

Calories 272 | Fat 15g (sat 10g) | Cholesterol 0mg | Carbs 33g | Total sugars 8g (added 0g) | Protein 5g | Fiber 7g | Sodium 509mg | Potassium 911mg. Nutrition bonus: Vitamin A (184% daily value) | Vitamin C (87% dv) | Iron (20% dv).

RIBOLLITA

Ribollita, a hearty Tuscan vegetable soup, uses day-old bread to add body. This version uses a bean mash instead, which keeps the soup gluten-free and adds fiber.

1 **14-ounce can whole peeled plum tomatoes**

2 **15-ounce cans cannellini beans, rinsed** (see Tip, opposite), **divided**

3 **tablespoons extra-virgin olive oil, divided**

1 **medium leek, halved lengthwise and sliced** (see Tip, page 197), **white and light green parts only**

¼ **cup thinly sliced garlic**

½ **teaspoon ground pepper, divided**

1 **cup diced carrots**

1 **cup diced celery**

1 **cup diced zucchini**

¼ **teaspoon salt, divided**

1 **bunch kale** or **chard, tough stems removed and cut into 2-inch-wide slices**

¼ **head Savoy** or **green cabbage, cut into 1-inch cubes (about 4 cups)**

2 **cups diced russet potatoes**

3 **cups vegetable broth**

2 **cups water**

½ **teaspoon dried thyme**

1 **bay leaf**

⅛ **teaspoon celery seeds**

Crushed red pepper to taste

1. Drain the tomatoes, reserving the liquid. Dice the tomatoes. Using a potato masher, mash half the beans into a paste. Set the tomatoes and beans aside.

2. Heat 2 tablespoons oil in a large pot over medium heat. Add leek and garlic; cook, stirring, until tender but not brown, 2 to 3 minutes. Season with ⅛ teaspoon pepper. Stir in carrots, celery, zucchini and the remaining 1 tablespoon oil; cook, stirring, until the vegetables are nearly tender, 3 to 5 minutes. Season with ⅛ teaspoon each salt and pepper.

3. Stir in kale (or chard) and cabbage. Cover and cook, stirring occasionally, until wilted, 4 to 6 minutes. Add potatoes, broth, water, tomatoes and juice, the mashed and whole beans, thyme and bay leaf. Bring to a simmer over medium heat. Add celery seeds, crushed red pepper and the remaining ¼ teaspoon pepper and ⅛ teaspoon salt. Cover and cook, stirring occasionally and reducing the heat to maintain a gentle simmer, until all the vegetables are tender, 15 to 20 minutes.

SERVES 8: ABOUT 1¾ CUPS EACH

Calories 211 | Fat 6g (sat 1g) | Cholesterol 0mg | Carbs 32g | Total sugars 6g (added 0g) | Protein 8g | Fiber 8g | Sodium 505mg | Potassium 669mg.
Nutrition bonus: Vitamin A (108% daily value) | Vitamin C (89% dv) | Folate (23% dv).

Give canned beans
a rinse before using to
reduce the sodium by
up to 35 percent, or opt
for low-sodium or
no-salt-added beans.

Save the rinds from your Parmesan cheese when the wedges are spent and add them to soups and stews (as is done here) for a flavor boost.

BAKED VEGETABLE SOUP

Originally prepared in the wood-burning hearths of Italian homes, this peasant-style soup is simple to make in a modern oven. Brimming with artichokes, mushrooms, zucchini and leeks, it heats up the house as it becomes the perfect warming meal.

5 tablespoons extra-virgin olive oil

1 pound Yukon Gold potatoes, halved and sliced ¼ inch thick

1½ teaspoons salt, divided

2 medium zucchini, halved and sliced ½ inch thick

2 medium leeks, white and light green parts only, thinly sliced (see Tip, page 197)

4 medium stalks celery, thinly sliced

10 ounces cremini (baby bella) mushrooms, quartered

4 cups frozen artichoke hearts (two 9-ounce boxes), thawed, or 10 fresh artichoke hearts, quartered

¼ cup chopped fresh parsley, plus more for garnish

1 15-ounce can no-salt-added diced tomatoes, with their juice

1 2-inch piece Parmesan cheese rind, plus finely shredded Parmesan for garnish

6 cups water

½ teaspoon ground pepper

1. Preheat oven to 350°F.

2. Pour oil into a large ovenproof pot (about 6-quart) and arrange potato slices in an even layer over the oil. Sprinkle with ¾ teaspoon salt. Layer in zucchini, leeks, celery, mushrooms, artichoke hearts and ¼ cup parsley; sprinkle with the remaining ¾ teaspoon salt. Pour tomatoes over the vegetables and nestle Parmesan rind into them. Add water (the vegetables will not be completely submerged), cover and bring to a boil over high heat.

3. Once boiling, transfer the pot to the oven and bake, covered, until the vegetables are tender, but still firm, 1 to 1¼ hours. Season with pepper and serve garnished with parsley and Parmesan, if desired.

SERVES 8: ABOUT 1¾ CUPS EACH

Calories 204 | Fat 10g (sat 1g) | Cholesterol 0mg | Carbs 26g | Total sugars 5g (added 0g) | Protein 5g | Fiber 7g | Sodium 529mg | Potassium 813mg.
Nutrition bonus: Vitamin C (45% daily value) | Folate (37% dv) | Vitamin A (26% dv).

VEGGISTRONE

The defining characteristic of any minestrone is that it is packed with vegetables. This makes a big pot of soup, so plan to freeze some—individual portions work well for lunches. Think of this recipe as a starting point for other healthy soup variations, too: toss in leftover chopped cooked chicken or whole-wheat pasta or brown rice to make it heartier.

- 2 tablespoons extra-virgin olive oil
- 2 cups chopped onions (2 medium)
- 2 cups chopped celery (4 medium stalks)
- 1 cup chopped green bell pepper (1 medium)
- 4 cloves garlic, minced
- 3 cups chopped cabbage
- 3 cups chopped cauliflower (about ½ medium)
- 2 cups chopped carrots (4 medium)
- 2 cups green beans, cut into 1-inch pieces, *or* frozen, thawed
- 8 cups low-sodium vegetable broth *or* chicken broth
- 2 cups water
- 1 15-ounce can tomato sauce
- 1 14-ounce can diced tomatoes
- 1 15-ounce can kidney *or* pinto beans, rinsed
- 1 bay leaf
- 4 cups chopped fresh spinach *or* one 10-ounce package frozen chopped spinach, thawed
- ½ cup thinly sliced fresh basil
- 10 tablespoons freshly grated Parmesan cheese

1. Heat oil in a large pot (8-quart or larger) over medium heat. Add onions, celery, bell pepper and garlic; cook, stirring frequently, until softened, 13 to 15 minutes. Add cabbage, cauliflower, carrots and green beans; cook, stirring occasionally, until slightly softened, about 10 minutes more.

2. Add broth, water, tomato sauce, tomatoes with their juices, beans and bay leaf; cover and bring to a boil. Reduce heat and simmer, partially covered, until the vegetables are tender, 20 to 25 minutes. Stir in spinach and simmer for 10 minutes more.

3. Discard the bay leaf. Stir in basil. Top each portion with 1 tablespoon cheese.

➤ **MAKE AHEAD:** Prepare through Step 2 and refrigerate for up to 5 days or freeze for up to 6 months; finish Step 3 just before serving.

SERVES 10: 2 CUPS EACH

Calories 162 | Fat 5g (sat 1g) | Cholesterol 4mg | Carbs 24g | Total sugars 10g (added 0g) | Protein 7g | Fiber 9g | Sodium 575mg | Potassium 769mg.
Nutrition bonus: Vitamin A (126% daily value) | Vitamin C (93% dv) | Folate (24% dv).

BETTER-THE-NEXT-DAY SOUPS

A big pot of soup almost always yields leftovers—and very often, the flavors are more intense or nuanced after sitting in the refrigerator overnight, as the ingredients get more acquainted and comfortable with each other. These soups are delicious the day they're made—but even finer the next.

NORMA'S MUSHROOM
BARLEY SOUP
P. 63

CUCUMBER-ALMOND GAZPACHO

Not all gazpachos are red. In this take on the chilled Spanish soup, we use cucumbers, yellow bell pepper and unsweetened almond milk for full-bodied and savory results.

 2 **English cucumbers, divided**

 2 **cups chopped yellow bell pepper, divided**

 2 **cups 1-inch pieces country-style whole-wheat bread (crusts removed)**

1½ **cups unsweetened almond milk**

 ½ **cup toasted slivered almonds, divided**

 5 **teaspoons extra-virgin olive oil, plus more for garnish**

 2 **teaspoons white-wine vinegar**

 1 **clove garlic**

 ½ **teaspoon salt**

1. Dice enough unpeeled cucumber to equal ½ cup and combine with ½ cup bell pepper; refrigerate.

2. Peel the remaining cucumbers and cut into chunks. Working in two batches, puree the peeled cucumber, the remaining bell pepper, bread, almond milk, 6 tablespoons almonds, oil, vinegar, garlic and salt in a blender until smooth. Transfer to a large bowl and refrigerate until chilled, at least 2 hours and up to 1 day.

3. To serve, garnish with the remaining 2 tablespoons almonds and the reserved vegetables. Drizzle with a little oil, if desired.

➤➤ **MAKE AHEAD:** Refrigerate diced vegetables (Step 1) and gazpacho (Step 2) separately for up to 1 day.

SERVES 5: 1 CUP EACH

Calories 201 | Fat 12g (sat 1g) | Cholesterol 0mg | Carbs 19g | Total sugars 5g (added 1g) | Protein 6g | Fiber 4g | Sodium 357mg | Potassium 435mg.
Nutrition bonus: Vitamin C (195% daily value).

THAI COCONUT CURRY SOUP

Thai soups often get their savory flavor from fish sauce. To keep this one vegetarian and add an umami note, we simmer dried shiitakes in vegetable broth.

- 6 cups low-sodium vegetable broth, divided
- ¾ ounce dried shiitake mushrooms
- 1 tablespoon extra-virgin olive oil
- 1½ cups chopped onion
- 2 teaspoons grated fresh ginger
- 2 jalapeño peppers, minced
- 1½ tablespoons Thai red curry paste (see Tip, page 120)
- 1½ tablespoons reduced-sodium tamari
- 1½ teaspoons lime zest
- ¼ cup lime juice
- ½ teaspoon salt
- 2¼ cups coconut milk
- 12 ounces diced extra-firm tofu (½-inch)
- 3 ounces fresh oyster mushrooms or other wild mushrooms, chopped
- 4 cups chopped mature spinach (5 ounces)
  Fresh cilantro for garnish

1. Combine 1 cup broth and dried shiitakes in a small saucepan. Bring to a boil over medium-high heat. Cover, reduce heat to maintain a simmer and cook for 10 minutes. Strain the broth through a coffee filter (or a double layer of cheesecloth) to catch the grit, and squeeze the mushrooms to extract as much liquid as possible. Reserve the cooking liquid and chop the mushrooms.

2. Heat oil in a large pot over medium-high heat. Add onion and cook, stirring frequently, until starting to brown, 2 to 4 minutes. Reduce heat to medium and continue cooking, stirring often, until the onion is soft, 3 to 5 minutes. Stir in the remaining 5 cups broth, scraping up any browned bits. Cover and bring to a boil over high heat. Add ginger, jalapeños, curry paste, tamari, lime zest and juice, salt and the reserved mushroom-cooking liquid. Cover and return to a boil.

3. Reduce heat to medium and add coconut milk, tofu, fresh mushrooms and the soaked shiitakes; return to a simmer and cook, partially covered, until the mushrooms are tender, 3 to 5 minutes. Stir in spinach and cook until wilted, 2 to 3 minutes more. Serve garnished with cilantro, if desired.

▶▶ **MAKE AHEAD:** Refrigerate for up to 5 days.

SERVES 8: ABOUT 1½ CUPS EACH

Calories 223 | Fat 18g (sat 13g) | Cholesterol 0mg | Carbs 12g | Total sugars 4g (added 0g) | Protein 7g | Fiber 3g | Sodium 473mg | Potassium 428mg.
Nutrition bonus: Vitamin A (29% daily value) | Vitamin C (23% dv) | Iron (22% dv).

INTO THE DEEP FREEZE

By Sara Berger

I inherited my mom's petite frame, her distaste for amaretto flavoring and her penchant for making ridiculously immense quantities of soup. Open either of our freezers and you'll find row upon row of stacked Tupperware—like we're preparing for some sort of Armageddon and only we know that soup will save us all.

Inside our well-stocked freezers, frost crystals form along edges of cloudy soup blocks, and nothing is labeled. For most, it would be a guessing game, but I can identify each one: There's the chicken noodle soup, with its dense matzo balls and bright orange rounds of carrots. Then there's the minestrone soup, and its twin sister, red chili—look closely for the green leafy kale to tell them apart. And then there is the grande dame of them all: mushroom barley.

It's my grandma's recipe. When she passed away at 92, one of my cousins got her gold heart bracelet, and my aunt wears her engagement diamond in a pendant necklace. Of course, jewelry is pretty, but the real gift she left us was her recipes. Specifically, her recipe for mushroom barley soup, simmered with a marrow bone until hauntingly rich and satisfying.

Considering the fact that my diet consisted mainly of buttered noodles and jelly beans when I was little, it seems odd to think that I'd be the first at the table when Grandma made her soup. Being one of eight grandchildren, however, it paid to be aggressive, and I wanted to be sure I got the prize: that marrow bone. Surrounded by the big sounds of family, my grandma would fish out the smooth, hot bone and ladle it with a thunk into my white-and-blue porcelain bowl. Picking up her gift, I'd purse my lips like a kiss to the spongy center and suck that bone dry.

My grandma's mushroom barley soup took time to prepare, and as she got older, it became too tiring for her to stand at the stove chopping, and stirring, and skimming the fat. She made it less often, and my mom began making it more. The result was a metaphorical passing of the ladle; my mom became the new queen. And in her reign, the unspoken rule was: "Soup forever."

It was also from them that I learned soup freezes miraculously well—and the freezer made my mom's rule become reality: we were never without batches of it. She would quadruple every recipe so that whenever a craving arose, we knew exactly where to look.

Even now, one husband, two kids and 20 years later, mushroom barley still reigns supreme in my book. "I made a really good batch last week," my mom tells me over the Bluetooth in our car as my family and I drive from Chicago to visit my parents' home in Michigan. She knows that the first thing we'll do when we stumble stiff-legged out of the car is ransack the kitchen. My kids will stand tippy-toed, uncovering candy from the pantry's top shelf. My husband will open the refrigerator and dig out the deli turkey. And I will open the freezer, use my ever-knowing eye to scan past the chicken noodle and find the mushroom barley. See, while my own freezer is similarly stocked, I've never made my grandma's mushroom barley. It's always been her—and my mom's—gift to me, and I prefer to keep it that way as long as possible.

I heat it up and it smells meaty and earthy and tastes like childhood and home. My mom watches as I eat. "I made it in such a big pot I had to stand on a chair to stir it," she says without the slightest bit of irony. It's comical to picture my mom standing on a chair, stirring a giant vat of soup. But the truth is, there is so much love in that mushroom barley there is barely a pot big enough to contain it.

SARA STILLMAN BERGER is a writer and mother living in New York City. Her most recent work has appeared in Martha Stewart Weddings, Brides Magazine, Modern Luxury, The Washington Post *and on* Scary Mommy.

ACTIVE   30 MIN
TOTAL   3 HRS

NORMA'S MUSHROOM BARLEY SOUP

Long-simmered marrow bones give this soup its luxurious flavor. The texture of the finished soup is hearty—bordering on a soupy risotto. *(Photo: page 56.)*

21 cups water, divided
4 beef marrow bones (about 1½ pounds)
2½ ounces mixed dried mushrooms (about 3 cups)
6 bone-in beef short ribs (about 2½ pounds)
1 large onion, chopped
3 6-ounce packages Manischewitz vegetable with mushrooms soup mix
1 cup pearl barley
2 large carrots, sliced
2 cups green beans, trimmed and halved
1½ cups corn, fresh *or* frozen
1 cup sliced fresh mushrooms
1 tablespoon kosher salt
1 teaspoon ground pepper
Sour cream & chives for serving

1. Bring 18 cups water to a boil in a large stockpot over high heat. Add marrow bones and reduce heat to medium. Cook for 20 minutes.

2. Meanwhile, soak dried mushrooms in the remaining 3 cups water in a small bowl for 20 minutes. Drain. Add the soaked mushrooms, short ribs and onion to the pot. Return to a boil, then reduce heat to maintain a simmer and cook for 1 hour.

3. Add Manischewitz soup mix and barley. Cook until the beef and the soup-mix beans are tender, about 1 hour more. Add carrots, green beans, corn, fresh mushrooms, salt and pepper; cook, stirring occasionally, until the vegetables are soft but not mushy, about 15 minutes more.

4. Remove the marrow bones and carefully scrape the marrow into the soup. Transfer the short ribs to a clean cutting board. Shred the meat from the bones with 2 forks and add back to the soup (discard the bones). Serve the soup topped with sour cream and chives, if desired.

➺ **MAKE AHEAD:** Refrigerate for up to 3 days or freeze for up to 3 months. Thin if necessary.

SERVES 14: 1½ CUPS EACH

Calories 332 | Fat 6g (sat 2g) | Cholesterol 25mg | Carbs 51g | Total sugars 5g (added 0g) | Protein 18g | Fiber 11g | Sodium 528mg | Potassium 532mg.
Nutrition bonus: Vitamin A (39% daily value) | Iron (20% dv).

If you don't happen to see marrow bones packaged in the meat case, ask the butcher—they almost always have them on hand.

CHIPOTLE ALBONDIGAS SOUP

Just a bit of spicy chorizo sausage adds lots of flavor to the meatballs in this hearty Mexican soup. Dandelion greens, carrots and corn are colorful additions.

4 cups low-sodium chicken *or* beef broth

4 cups water

1-2 limes, divided

4 ounces fresh chorizo, casing removed (1-2 links)

½ cup fine whole-grain cornmeal (*see Tip*)

½ cup finely chopped scallions

½ cup finely chopped fresh cilantro

1 large egg

2 cloves garlic, minced

1 teaspoon dried oregano

¼ teaspoon ground pepper

1¼ pounds lean (90% *or* leaner) ground beef *or* bison

6 cups chopped dandelion greens *or* chard, tough stems removed

1 cup sliced carrots

1-2 chipotle chiles in adobo sauce, minced

1 cup corn kernels, fresh *or* frozen

1. Bring broth and water to a simmer in a large pot over medium heat.

2. Meanwhile, zest and juice 1 lime; reserve the juice. Break up chorizo in a large bowl. Mix in cornmeal, scallions, cilantro, egg, garlic, oregano, pepper and the lime zest. Add meat. Gently mix to combine (do not overmix). Using 1 tablespoon for each, make about 40 small meatballs.

3. Add greens, carrots and chipotle to taste to the simmering broth mixture, then add the meatballs. Simmer until the meatballs are cooked through and the vegetables are tender, 10 to 12 minutes. Stir in corn and cook until heated through, 1 to 2 minutes more. Stir in 2 tablespoons lime juice. Serve with lime wedges, if desired.

➤➤ **MAKE AHEAD:** Refrigerate for up to 3 days.

SERVES 6: ABOUT 2 CUPS EACH

Calories 390 | Fat 20g (sat 7g) | Cholesterol 109mg | Carbs 24g | Total sugars 4g (added 0g) | Protein 31g | Fiber 4g | Sodium 441mg | Potassium 958mg. Nutrition bonus: Vitamin A (189% daily value) | Vitamin C (47% dv) | Vitamin B$_{12}$ (45% dv) | Iron (30% dv).

All cornmeal is not created equal. Whole-grain cornmeal has the nutritious germ intact. If the label says it has been degermed, it's not whole grain.

LOW-CALORIE • GLUTEN-FREE

ACTIVE 1 HR
TOTAL 1½ HRS

KIELBASA *and* CABBAGE SOUP

This soup (called *kapusniak* in Polish) is traditionally made with sauerkraut. To keep the sodium in check, we use fresh cabbage and save the sauerkraut for a deliciously salty-sour garnish. Toast the caraway seeds in a small dry skillet over medium heat, shaking frequently, for 1 to 2 minutes; let cool before grinding.

8 ounces kielbasa
2 tablespoons extra-virgin olive oil
2 cups chopped onion
2 cups diced carrot
¾ cup diced celery
2 large cloves garlic, minced
8 cups quartered and thinly sliced cabbage (about 1 pound)
8 cups low-sodium chicken broth
4 cups diced peeled russet potatoes
¼ cup chopped fresh dill
1½ teaspoons caraway seeds, toasted and ground
1½ teaspoons smoked paprika
¾ teaspoon ground pepper
½ teaspoon salt
2 tablespoons white-wine vinegar
Fresh sauerkraut *and/or* sour cream for serving

1. Cut kielbasa in half lengthwise, then crosswise into ¼-inch-thick slices. Cook in a large pot over medium-high heat, stirring, until browned and the fat has rendered, about 5 minutes. Transfer to a plate with a slotted spoon.

2. Add oil, onion, carrot and celery to the pot and cook, stirring often, until starting to brown, about 5 minutes. Reduce heat to medium and continue cooking, stirring often, until the vegetables are soft, about 4 minutes more. Add garlic and cook, stirring, for 1 minute. Add cabbage and cook, stirring occasionally, until slightly wilted, about 3 minutes.

3. Add broth, potatoes, dill, caraway, paprika, pepper and salt. Cover and bring to a boil. Reduce heat to maintain a simmer and cook, uncovered, until the potatoes are tender, about 30 minutes. Stir in vinegar and the kielbasa. Serve topped with sauerkraut and/or sour cream, if desired.

➤➤ **MAKE AHEAD:** Refrigerate for up to 4 days.

SERVES 8: ABOUT 1½ CUPS EACH

Calories 222 | Fat 7g (sat 2g) | Cholesterol 13mg | Carbs 31g | Total sugars 7g (added 0g) | Protein 12g | Fiber 5g | Sodium 509mg | Potassium 847mg.
Nutrition bonus: Vitamin A (114% daily value) | Vitamin C (59% dv).

BETTER-THE-NEXT-DAY SOUPS **67**

POT ROAST SOUP

Plenty of veggies—and of course meat and potatoes—guarantee that this ode to the classic Sunday supper will satisfy even the hungriest diners.

2 pounds boneless beef chuck roast, cut into 1-inch pieces

1½ teaspoons kosher salt, divided

½ teaspoon ground pepper

1 tablespoon extra-virgin olive oil

1 cup dry red wine (see Tip)

6 medium red potatoes, cut into 1-inch pieces

2 cups chopped onions

2 large carrots, chopped

1 cup sliced baby bella (cremini) or white mushrooms

1 15-ounce can fire-roasted crushed tomatoes

3 cloves garlic, minced

4 cups low-sodium beef broth

2 sprigs fresh thyme

1 bay leaf

½ cup reduced-fat sour cream

¼ teaspoon ground pepper

1. Season beef with 1 teaspoon salt and pepper. Heat oil in a large pot over medium-high heat. Add the beef and cook until browned on all sides, about 4 minutes. Add wine and bring to boil, scraping up browned bits. Add potatoes, onions, carrots and mushrooms. Cook, stirring occasionally, for 1 minute. Add tomatoes, with their juices, and garlic. Cook, stirring occasionally, for 1 minute.

2. Add broth, thyme, bay leaf and the remaining ½ teaspoon salt. Bring to a boil. Reduce heat to a simmer, cover and cook until the beef is tender, about 1½ hours.

3. Whisk sour cream and pepper in a small bowl. Serve the soup topped with the sour cream.

➤➤ **MAKE AHEAD:** Refrigerate for up to 4 days.

SERVES 8: 1½ CUPS EACH

Calories 483 | Fat 20g (sat 8g) | Cholesterol 99mg | Carbs 37g | Total sugars 7g (added 0g) | Protein 32g | Fiber 5g | Sodium 616mg | Potassium 1,239mg.
Nutrition bonus: Vitamin A (67% daily value) | Vitamin C (43% dv) | Vitamin B$_{12}$ (31% dv) | Iron (23% dv).

Water or additional broth may be substituted for the red wine, if you like.

SINGAPORE-STYLE CHICKEN *AND* NOODLE SOUP

Serve this flavorful soup with hot sauce and lime wedges, if desired. Look for bean thread noodles, sometimes labeled vermicelli, mung bean or cellophane noodles, in the Asian section of large supermarkets or at an Asian market. After preparing them, rinse well to prevent sticking.

- 2 cups chopped onions
- 2 small red *or* green chiles (such as serrano *or* jalapeño), seeded and diced
- 1 2-inch piece fresh ginger, peeled and coarsely chopped
- 2 cloves garlic, crushed
- ¼ cup macadamia nuts
- 3 tablespoons fish sauce
- 2 teaspoons dark brown sugar
- 1 tablespoon ground coriander
- 2 teaspoons ground cumin
- 1 teaspoon curry powder
- 1 teaspoon ground turmeric
- 1 teaspoon ground *or* crushed fennel seed
- 1 teaspoon ground pepper
- 2 tablespoons peanut oil
- 6 cups low-sodium chicken broth
- 1 pound boneless, skinless chicken breast, trimmed
- 1 14-ounce can "lite" coconut milk
- 2 tablespoons lime juice, or to taste
- 2 tablespoons reduced-sodium soy sauce
- 1 14-ounce package extra-firm tofu, drained, cut into ½-inch cubes
- 1 cup diced tomatoes *or* one 14-ounce can diced tomatoes, drained
- 1 7-ounce package mung bean sprouts (3 cups)

- 8 ounces bean thread noodles
- 3 hard-boiled eggs, thinly sliced
- 6 scallions, thinly sliced
- ½ cup coarsely chopped fresh cilantro

1. Put onions, chiles, ginger, garlic, nuts, fish sauce, brown sugar, coriander, cumin, curry powder, turmeric, fennel and pepper in a blender. Puree until the mixture forms a paste.

2. Heat oil in a large pot over medium heat. Scrape in the paste with a spatula and cook, stirring, until it starts to color, 3 to 5 minutes. Add broth and chicken and bring to a simmer. Simmer, turning the chicken once or twice, for 10 minutes. Stir in coconut milk, lime juice and soy sauce; simmer for 5 minutes more.

3. Remove the chicken and shred with two forks. Add tofu, tomatoes and bean sprouts to the soup and cook for 2 minutes. Stir in the shredded chicken.

4. Prepare noodles according to package directions.

5. Divide the noodles among 8 soup bowls. Ladle the soup over and top with egg slices, scallions and cilantro.

▸▸ **MAKE AHEAD:** Refrigerate noodles, soup and toppings in separate containers (so the noodles don't soak up all the liquid) for up to 2 days.

SERVES 8: 1⅔ CUPS SOUP & ¾ CUP NOODLES EACH

Calories 412 | Fat 17g (sat 5g) | Cholesterol 101mg | Carbs 42g | Total sugars 6g (added 1g) | Protein 26g | Fiber 4g | Sodium 714mg | Potassium 585mg.
Nutrition bonus: Vitamin C (23% daily value) | Iron (21% dv).

TURKISH CHICKPEA *AND* LAMB SOUP

Dried chickpeas in this recipe act like sponges, soaking up flavorful liquids while the soup cooks and even while the leftovers sit in the fridge. The pistachio-mint pesto adds another layer of flavor.

¾ cup dried chickpeas, soaked in cold water to cover for 8 to 24 hours

3 teaspoons extra-virgin olive oil, divided

1 large onion, chopped

2 medium carrots, diced

3 cloves garlic, minced

2 teaspoons ground cumin

1 teaspoon ground coriander

¼ teaspoon cayenne pepper

1 1-pound lamb shank, trimmed

½ teaspoon salt

¼ teaspoon ground pepper

4 cups low-sodium chicken broth

1 14-ounce can diced tomatoes

2 bay leaves

½ cup bulgur, rinsed

2 tablespoons lemon juice

PISTACHIO-MINT PESTO

1½ cups fresh mint

⅓ cup shelled pistachios

2 cloves garlic, crushed and peeled

2 tablespoons extra-virgin olive oil

2 tablespoons lemon juice

2 tablespoons low-fat plain yogurt

⅛ teaspoon salt (optional)

1. To prepare soup: Drain chickpeas; set aside.

2. Heat 2 teaspoons oil in a large pot over medium-high heat. Add onion and carrots; cook, stirring, until softened, 3 to 5 minutes. Add minced garlic, cumin, coriander and cayenne; cook, stirring, until fragrant, about 20 seconds. Remove from heat.

3. Sprinkle lamb shank with salt and pepper. Heat the remaining 1 teaspoon oil in a medium cast-iron skillet over medium heat. Add the lamb and cook, turning occasionally, until browned all over, 3 to 7 minutes.

4. Transfer the lamb to the pot. Add broth, tomatoes, bay leaves and the chickpeas. Bring to a boil. Reduce heat to maintain a simmer, cover and cook until the lamb and chickpeas are very tender, 1¾ to 2¼ hours.

5. Meanwhile, place bulgur in a medium bowl. Cover with boiling water and let stand for 15 minutes. Drain in a sieve, pressing out excess water.

6. To prepare pesto: Combine mint, pistachios and garlic in a food processor and process until finely chopped. With the motor running, gradually add oil, lemon juice and yogurt. Process until a paste forms. If using unsalted pistachios, add salt, if desired.

7. Skim fat from the surface of the soup. Using tongs, transfer the lamb to a clean cutting board. Coarsely shred the meat and return it to the soup. (Discard the bone.) Add the drained bulgur. Heat the soup until heated through. Stir in lemon juice. Top each serving with pesto.

➤➤ **MAKE AHEAD:** Refrigerate for up to 2 days. Thin with broth or water, if necessary, when reheating.

SERVES 6: ABOUT 1⅔ CUPS EACH

Calories 344 | Fat 14g (sat 2g) | Cholesterol 22mg | Carbs 38g | Total sugars 8g (added 0g) | Protein 20g | Fiber 10g | Sodium 440mg | Potassium 747mg. Nutrition bonus: Vitamin A (93% daily value) | Vitamin C (38% dv) | Iron (34% dv).

VERY GREEN
LENTIL SOUP
P.79

GREEN SOUPS

Soup inherently makes you feel good—but these gorgeously hued soups make you feel really, really good! To make green soup, simply use any (and as many) green vegetables as you like. That's about the only rule that defines a green soup as far as we can tell. Puree it if you want a creamy soup or leave it chunky. Add a topping—cheese, fresh herbs, a swirl of olive oil—or not. Sip, slurp and feel beautiful and virtuous!

BASIC GREEN SOUP

This chard and spinach soup gets complex flavor from caramelized onions as well as lemon juice; a sprinkle of rice gives it body and velvety texture. Serve with a swirl of extra-virgin olive oil for richness.

- 2 tablespoons extra-virgin olive oil, plus more for garnish
- 2 large yellow onions, chopped
- ¾ teaspoon salt, divided
- 2 tablespoons water plus 3 cups, divided
- ¼ cup arborio rice
- 1 bunch green chard (about 1 pound)
- 14 cups gently packed spinach (about 12 ounces), trimmed
- 4 cups low-sodium vegetable broth
  Big pinch of cayenne pepper
- 1 tablespoon lemon juice, or more to taste

1. Heat 2 tablespoons oil in a large skillet over high heat. Add onions and ¼ teaspoon salt; cook, stirring frequently, until the onions begin to brown, about 5 minutes. Reduce the heat to low, add 2 tablespoons water and cover. Cook, stirring frequently until the pan cools down, then occasionally, always covering the pan again, until the onions are a deep caramel color, 25 to 30 minutes.

2. Meanwhile, combine the remaining 3 cups water, ½ teaspoon salt and rice in a large pot. Bring to a boil. Reduce heat to maintain a simmer, cover and cook for 15 minutes. Strip ribs from chard (save for another use, if desired) and coarsely chop leaves. Coarsely chop spinach.

3. When the rice has cooked for 15 minutes, stir in the chard. Return to a simmer; cover and cook for 10 minutes. When the onions are caramelized, stir a little of the simmering liquid into them, then add them to the rice along with the spinach, broth and cayenne. Return to a simmer, cover and cook, stirring once, until the spinach is tender but still bright green, about 5 minutes more.

4. Puree the soup with an immersion blender or in a regular blender, in batches, until smooth. (Use caution when blending hot liquids.) Stir in lemon juice. Garnish each serving with a drizzle of olive oil.

▸▸ **MAKE AHEAD:** Prepare through Step 4 (omitting the lemon juice) and refrigerate for up to 3 days. Season with lemon juice and garnish with oil just before serving.

SERVES 8: ABOUT 1¼ CUPS EACH

Calories 95 | Fat 4g (sat 1g) | Cholesterol 0mg | Carbs 13g | Total sugars 3g (added 0g) | Protein 3g | Fiber 3g | Sodium 447mg | Potassium 510mg.
Nutrition bonus: Vitamin A (149% daily value) | Vitamin C (54% dv) | Folate (24% dv).

GOING GREEN

By Anna Thomas

It was a gray-sky day in the San Bernardino Mountains, and outside the cabin a bitter wind was swatting down the last damp leaves. I needed to put myself in a better mood—and to lose a few pounds. So I went down to the farmers' market, picked up bunches of the dark greens that thrive in cool weather—great shiny leaves of chard, spinach, kale, Italian parsley and cilantro—and started to chop. I threw some sliced onion into hot olive oil and heard the happy sizzle. I added garlic. Soon the cabin was filled with that greatest of perfumes. My spirits were already lifting.

The washed greens went into another pot with water and sea salt and a diced potato. When the onions, slowly sizzling in the skillet, turned the color of caramel toffee, in they went to the soup pot. A pinch of red pepper flakes, a splash of lemon juice and I pureed the soup.

So easy. So green. And *so delicious*.

I ate that first steaming bowlful, and I sat up straighter and grinned wide. I was infused with phytochemicals, those mysterious good-for-you compounds that I didn't completely understand. Did I realize then that green soup would change my life? No, but over the next week it was green soup for lunch, more for a break while working, and then a bowl of green for dinner, dressed up with croutons or crumbles of moist feta cheese—divine. I had my new diet plan: more green, less everything else.

Soon everyone in the family was eating it, even my kids, even their friends. I hauled back larger loads of greens—mustard greens, cavolo nero kale, leeks. I made green soup every week, no two alike but every one following that original template. I used rice instead of potato, watercress and spinach instead of chard and kale. The formula seemed bulletproof: a pile of leafy greens, some slowly cooked onion for sweetness, a little something starchy for body and that pop of cayenne and lemon to finish.

One night friends were coming for dinner. By then, I was back in my skinny jeans and green soup was my steady date; I decided it should come out to a party. I had some mushrooms, so I sautéed them with garlic and thyme until they were dark as mahogany, added them to the simmering greens and pureed it all to a velvety cream. That soup was earthy, mysterious, a bit smoky from a touch of Spanish paprika. The next day people were calling for the recipe. This should have tipped me off about what was to come.

Many pots of soup later, I wrote about green soup for the *Los Angeles Times*, and the avalanche was unleashed. Emails—a trickle, then a flood. *I love that green soup…. I used to make one with turnip greens…. My version has broccoli…. I lived on parsley soup all through graduate school….* The world loved green soup and wanted to talk about it. I'd never had such an outpouring of responses. Some had a positively religious fervor. *Green soup is in the house. Hallelujah!*

I probably cooked 40 or 50 different green soups over the next decade, posting the recipes on my website. The emails kept coming. When I began writing my book, *Love Soup*, I knew I'd have to have a chapter devoted to green soups. But it turned out that one chapter wouldn't be enough. I wound up with one for fall and winter soups, one for spring and summer. And new inspirations keep on coming.

The green soups here take green to another level—into the exotic scent of green curry, the hearty pairing of Le Puy lentils, the luxury of spinach and chèvre in a bisque and the pure rustic pleasure of Baker's Pasta, which is loaded with parsley, walnuts and garlic, re-imagined as soup. Green, green—not so much a soup as a way of life. Hallelujah!

ANNA THOMAS wrote her first cookbook, The Vegetarian Epicure (1972), *while she was a film student at UCLA. Her book* Love Soup *won a James Beard award in 2010. Her most recent book is* Vegan Vegetarian Omnivore: Dinner for Everyone at the Table.

VERY GREEN LENTIL SOUP

Both French green lentils and the more commonly available brown lentils are delicious in this soup. Green lentils will hold their shape, while brown will start to break down a bit. *(Photo: page 74.)*

2 tablespoons extra-virgin olive oil, plus more for garnish

2 large yellow onions, chopped

1¼ teaspoons salt, divided

2 tablespoons water plus 4 cups, divided

1 cup French green (Le Puy) *or* brown lentils

8 large green chard leaves

1 medium Yukon Gold potato, scrubbed

12 cups gently packed spinach (about 10 ounces), any tough stems trimmed

4 scallions, cut into 1-inch pieces

5 cups low-sodium vegetable broth

2 cups chopped broccoli

1 tablespoon cumin seeds, lightly toasted and ground (*see Tip*)

½ teaspoon ground coriander

1 cup chopped fresh cilantro

2 tablespoons chopped fresh mint

½ jalapeño pepper, minced

Ground pepper to taste

1 tablespoon fresh lemon juice, or more to taste

Crumbled feta cheese for garnish

1. Heat oil in a large skillet over high heat. Add onions and ¼ teaspoon salt; cook, stirring frequently, until beginning to brown, about 5 minutes. Reduce heat to low, add 2 tablespoons water and cover. Cook, stirring frequently until the pan cools down, and then occasionally, always covering the pan again, until the onions are a deep caramel color, 25 to 35 minutes.

2. Meanwhile, rinse lentils and combine with the remaining 4 cups water in a large pot. Bring to a boil. Reduce heat to maintain a simmer, cover and cook for 20 minutes. Trim the white ribs out of the chard; chop the greens and slice the ribs (keep in separate piles). Cut potato into ½-inch dice. Chop spinach; set aside.

3. When the lentils have cooked for 20 minutes, stir in the chard ribs, potato, scallions, broth and the remaining 1 teaspoon salt; return to a gentle simmer. Cover and cook for 15 minutes.

4. Stir in the chard leaves, broccoli, cumin and coriander. Stir a little of the simmering liquid into the caramelized onions, then add them to the soup. Return to a simmer, cover and cook 5 minutes more. Stir in the reserved spinach, cilantro, mint, jalapeño and pepper; return to a simmer, cover and cook until the spinach is tender but still bright green, about 5 minutes. Stir in lemon juice. Serve with a drizzle of olive oil and crumbled feta cheese, if desired.

▸▸ **MAKE AHEAD:** Refrigerate for up to 3 days.

SERVES 8: ABOUT 1⅔ CUPS EACH

Calories 181 | Fat 4g (sat 1g) | Cholesterol 0mg | Carbs 29g | Total sugars 5g (added 0g) | Protein 9g | Fiber 9g | Sodium 535mg | Potassium 793mg.
Nutrition bonus: Vitamin A (100% daily value) | Folate (51% dv) | Vitamin C (47% dv) | Iron (30% dv).

Toasting spices before grinding intensifies their flavor. Toast cumin seeds in a dry skillet over medium heat until fragrant, 1 to 2 minutes. Cool, then grind in a spice mill, blender or clean coffee grinder. No grinder? Use an equal amount of ground cumin.

SPINACH AND GOAT CHEESE BISQUE

A little fresh goat cheese and a touch of butter are just enough to make this spinach soup silky, creamy and a little nutty—but not enough to overdo it. We use dark green spinach for this soup because of the lovely color it produces, though you could use red-veined spinach and have just as good a flavor in a more Army-inspired khaki color.

- 1 tablespoon plus 1 teaspoon extra-virgin olive oil
- 2 large yellow onions, chopped
- ½ teaspoon salt, divided, plus more to taste
- 2 tablespoons plus 2 cups water, divided
- 1 teaspoon dried thyme *or* 2 teaspoons fresh
- 1 large Yukon Gold potato, peeled and diced
- 2 tablespoons cream sherry *or* Marsala
- 4 cups low-sodium vegetable broth
- 24 cups gently packed spinach (about 1¼ pounds), any tough stems trimmed
- Pinch of cayenne pepper
- ¼ teaspoon ground nutmeg
- ½ cup crumbled fresh goat cheese (2 ounces), plus more for garnish
- 2 tablespoons butter
- 1 tablespoon fresh lemon juice, or more to taste
- Soup croutons for garnish (see *Tip, opposite*)

1. Heat oil in a large skillet over high heat. Add onions and ¼ teaspoon salt; cook, stirring frequently, until the onions begin to brown, about 5 minutes. Reduce the heat to low, add 2 tablespoons water and thyme and cover. Cook, stirring frequently until the pan cools down, and then occasionally, always covering the pan again, until the onions are greatly reduced and have a deep caramel color, 25 to 30 minutes.

2. Meanwhile, combine the remaining 2 cups water and ¼ teaspoon salt in a large pot; add potato. Bring to a boil. Reduce heat to maintain a simmer and cook until very soft, 12 to 15 minutes.

3. When the onions are caramelized, stir sherry (or Marsala) into them; add them to the pot along with broth. Return to a simmer. Stir in spinach, cayenne and nutmeg; cover and cook, stirring once, until the spinach is tender but still bright green, about 5 minutes.

4. Remove from the heat, stir in goat cheese, butter and 1 tablespoon lemon juice; allow the butter and cheese to melt. Puree the soup in the pot with an immersion blender until perfectly smooth or in a regular blender in batches. (Use caution when blending hot liquids.) Taste and add more salt and/or lemon juice, if desired. Serve garnished with a soup crouton and crumbled goat cheese, if desired.

▸▸ **MAKE AHEAD:** Refrigerate for up to 3 days.

SERVES 8: ABOUT 1 CUP EACH

Calories 141 | Fat 7g (sat 3g) | Cholesterol 13mg | Carbs 16g | Total sugars 4g (added 0g) | Protein 4g | Fiber 4g | Sodium 291mg | Potassium 514mg.
Nutrition bonus: Vitamin A (118% daily value) | Vitamin C (30% dv) | Folate (24% dv).

To make croutons like these, cut ½-inch slices from a whole-grain baguette. Brush both sides with melted butter or extra-virgin olive oil and bake at 350°F until golden brown, 10 to 20 minutes.

GREEN CURRY SOUP

Mushrooms add meatiness to this chunky soup packed with spinach, green beans and broccoli and flavored with Thai curry paste—green, of course!

2 medium yellow onions

2 tablespoons extra-virgin olive oil plus 2 teaspoons, divided

½ teaspoon salt, divided

2 tablespoons Thai green curry paste (see Tip, page 120)

4-5 cups low-sodium vegetable broth

8 cups spinach (about 6 ounces), tough stems trimmed, divided

2 cups water

2 large cloves garlic, chopped

2½ cups shiitake or oyster mushrooms (about 4 ounces), cut into ¼-inch strips

1½ cups chopped green beans (1-inch)

1 cup thinly sliced peeled broccoli stems

5 scallions, sliced

1 tablespoon minced lemongrass

1 cup chopped fresh cilantro

1 serrano chile, finely chopped

2 tablespoons fresh lemon juice

Use a vegetable peeler to remove the tough outer layer of the broccoli stems before slicing.

1. Quarter onions lengthwise, then thinly slice crosswise. Heat 2 tablespoons oil in a large pot over medium-high heat. Add onions and ¼ teaspoon salt; cook, stirring often, until beginning to brown, 6 to 8 minutes. Stir in curry paste; cook, stirring, for 3 minutes. Stir in 4 cups broth; bring to a simmer.

2. Meanwhile, coarsely chop 4 cups spinach. Puree the remaining 4 cups spinach with water in a blender until it is chopped to confetti.

3. Heat the remaining 2 teaspoons oil in a large skillet over medium heat. Add garlic; cook, stirring, until fragrant, about 30 seconds. Add mushrooms; cook, stirring, until the liquid evaporates and the mushrooms color, 4 to 6 minutes.

4. Stir the mushrooms and green beans into the pot; simmer for 5 minutes. Stir in broccoli stems, scallions and lemongrass; simmer for 3 minutes more. Stir in chopped and pureed spinach, cilantro and a big pinch of serrano. Return to a simmer, cover and cook 1 minute. Add up to 1 cup of the remaining broth, if desired. Add lemon juice. Season with more salt, serrano and/or lemon juice to taste.

SERVES 6: ABOUT 1⅔ CUPS EACH

Calories 118 | Fat 7g (sat 1g) | Cholesterol 0mg | Carbs 13g | Total sugars 5g (added 0g) | Protein 3g | Fiber 4g | Sodium 417mg | Potassium 457mg.
Nutrition bonus: Vitamin A (60% daily value) | Vitamin C (35% dv) | Folate (20% dv).

GREEN SOUP WITH YAMS & SAGE

The rosy-skinned, light-fleshed Japanese yam is more dry and starchy than the typical orange sweet potato. While it gives this soup a nice texture, any sweet potato can be used.

3 tablespoons extra-virgin olive oil, divided, plus more for garnish

2 large onions, chopped

¾ teaspoon salt, divided

2 tablespoons plus 4 cups water, divided

4 cloves garlic, sliced

1 teaspoon chopped fresh thyme leaves or ½ teaspoon dried

1 large bunch Tuscan, lacinato *or* Russian kale

2 medium *or* 1 very large Japanese yam *or* regular sweet potato (about 1¼ pounds)

14 cups gently packed spinach (about 12 ounces), any tough stems trimmed

8 fresh sage leaves *or* 1 teaspoon crumbled dried

4 cups low-sodium vegetable broth

Pinch of cayenne pepper

Ground pepper to taste

1 tablespoon fresh lemon juice, or more to taste

1 tablespoon agave nectar, or more to taste (optional)

16 fried sage leaves for garnish (see *Tip, opposite*)

1. Heat 2 tablespoons oil in a large skillet over high heat. Add onions and ¼ teaspoon salt; cook, stirring frequently, until the onions are beginning to brown, about 5 minutes. Reduce the heat to low, stir in 2 tablespoons water, garlic and thyme and cover. Cook, stirring frequently until the pan cools down, and then occasionally, always covering the pan again, until the onions are greatly reduced and have a deep caramel color, 25 to 35 minutes.

2. Meanwhile, remove tough stems and ribs from kale and coarsely chop the greens. Peel yam (or sweet potato) and dice into 1-inch pieces. Coarsely chop spinach; set aside.

3. Combine the remaining 4 cups water and ½ teaspoon salt in a large pot; add the kale, yam (or sweet potato) and sage. Bring to a boil. Reduce heat to maintain a simmer, cover and cook for 15 minutes.

4. Stir in the spinach, return to a simmer, cover and cook, stirring once, for 10 minutes more. When the onions are caramelized, stir a little of the simmering liquid into them; add to the soup. Add broth; return to a simmer, cover and cook for 5 minutes more.

5. Puree the soup in the pot with an immersion blender until perfectly smooth or in a regular blender in batches. (Use caution when blending hot liquids.) Stir in cayenne, a few grinds of pepper and 1 tablespoon lemon juice. If the soup is too sweet for your taste, add more lemon juice; if it's too tart, add agave nectar, if desired. Just before serving, whisk the remaining 1 tablespoon oil into the hot soup. Garnish each bowl of soup with a drizzle of oil and 2 fried sage leaves, if desired.

SERVES 8: ABOUT 1½ CUPS EACH

Calories 134 | Fat 6g (sat 1g) | Cholesterol 0mg | Carbs 19g | Total sugars 5g (added 0g) | Protein 3g | Fiber 4g | Sodium 361mg | Potassium 534mg.
Nutrition bonus: Vitamin A (295% daily value) | Vitamin C (46% dv) | Folate (25% dv).

For fried sage leaves, heat ½ inch olive oil in a small saucepan over medium-high heat. Add sage leaves; fry just until crisp, 1 to 3 minutes. Remove with a slotted spoon and drain on a paper towel.

ARUGULA-ZUCCHINI VICHYSSOISE

This version of the French potato-and-leek soup is whisper-light and a lovely green color because we swap zucchini for the potatoes. Serve chilled or hot.

1 tablespoon extra-virgin olive oil

1 tablespoon butter

2 large leeks, white and pale green parts only, halved lengthwise, rinsed and thinly sliced

2 cloves garlic, minced

6 cups low-sodium chicken broth

4 cups chopped zucchini

¾ teaspoon salt

¼ teaspoon ground pepper

10 cups baby arugula

½ cup chopped fresh parsley

2 tablespoons lemon juice

1. Heat oil and butter in a large pot over medium heat. Add leeks and garlic. Cook, stirring, until softened but not browned, about 3 minutes. Stir in broth, zucchini, salt and pepper. Bring to a boil. Reduce heat, cover and simmer until the zucchini is tender, about 15 minutes. Remove from heat. Stir in arugula and let stand 5 minutes.

2. Puree the soup in the pot with an immersion blender or in batches in a regular blender. (Use caution when blending hot liquids.) Stir in parsley and lemon juice. Serve hot or chilled.

SERVES 6: 1½ CUPS EACH

Calories 148 | Fat 6g (sat 2g) | Cholesterol 5mg | Carbs 17g | Total sugars 6g (added 0g) | Protein 9g | Fiber 3g | Sodium 405mg | Potassium 568mg.
Nutrition bonus: Vitamin C (68% daily value) | Vitamin A (66% dv).

RUSTIC PARSLEY *AND* ORZO SOUP WITH WALNUTS

This soup is based on a traditional Italian dish that consists of lots of parsley, garlic, chopped walnuts, hot chile and olive oil, all fried up and tossed with pasta. We amped up the greens, made the pasta more of a supporting player and turned the recipe into a soup. It's best served immediately, because the orzo will absorb liquid as the soup is held. Or, if you plan to have leftovers, keep some of the orzo separate and add it as you reheat the soup.

1¼ cups whole-wheat orzo (8 ounces)

1 teaspoon extra-virgin olive oil plus 2 tablespoons, divided, plus more for garnish

1 large yellow onion, chopped

¾ teaspoon salt, divided, plus a pinch

10 cups gently packed spinach (about 8 ounces), any tough stems trimmed

2 large bunches parsley

1 medium Yukon Gold potato

5 cups low-sodium vegetable broth

2 cups water

2 tablespoons finely chopped garlic

1 cup finely chopped walnuts

½ teaspoon crushed red pepper

1 tablespoon fresh lemon juice, or more to taste

Ground pepper to taste

1 cup diced fresh tomatoes

1. Cook orzo in a saucepan of boiling water until almost tender, 8 to 9 minutes. Drain; rinse with cool water. Return to the pot and toss with 1 teaspoon oil; set aside.

2. Heat 1 tablespoon oil in a medium skillet over high heat. Add onion and ¼ teaspoon salt; reduce heat to medium-low, cover and cook, stirring frequently, always covering the pan again, until the onion is translucent and beginning to color, 10 to 15 minutes.

3. Coarsely chop spinach. Coarsely chop enough parsley to equal about 4 cups. Set aside 3 cups and finely chop the remaining 1 cup; set aside separately.

4. Peel and dice potato. Combine in a large pot with ½ teaspoon salt, broth, water and the sautéed onion. Bring to a boil over high heat. Reduce heat to maintain a simmer and cook for 12 minutes. Stir in the spinach and the 3 cups parsley; return to a simmer, cover and cook for 3 minutes more.

5. Meanwhile, heat the remaining 1 tablespoon oil in the skillet over medium heat. Add garlic and let it sizzle for about 45 seconds. Add walnuts and cook, stirring and watching carefully to prevent burning, for about 3 minutes. Stir in the remaining 1 cup parsley and crushed red pepper; cook, stirring, for 2 minutes more. Remove from heat.

6. Stir the cooked orzo into the soup, then stir in the parsley-walnut mixture. Season with lemon juice and pepper. Return the soup to a simmer.

7. Combine tomatoes with the remaining pinch of salt in a small bowl. Garnish each serving with a spoonful of the tomatoes and a drizzle of oil, if desired.

SERVES 6: ABOUT 1¾ CUPS EACH

Calories 393 | Fat 19g (sat 2g) | Cholesterol 0mg | Carbs 47g | Total sugars 5g (added 0g) | Protein 11g | Fiber 12g | Sodium 491mg | Potassium 793mg.
Nutrition bonus: Vitamin A (145% daily value) | Vitamin C (123% dv) | Folate (42% dv) | Iron (27% dv).

For the most perfect avocados, buy when firm and let them ripen at room temperature for a few days before using. They'll be less likely to bruise in transport when they're firm.

GREEN GAZPACHO

Make this cold soup in the middle of summer, when garden tomatoes, cucumbers and peppers are at their peak. Start with 1 cup of broth, adding more to reach the desired consistency. Very ripe (and juicy) summer tomatoes will need less broth—less-ripe tomatoes will need more.

2 medium tomatillos (8 ounces), husked, rinsed and coarsely chopped

2 medium heirloom green tomatoes, such as Zebra, *or* yellow tomatoes (8 ounces), coarsely chopped

¾ cup chopped seeded peeled cucumber

1 small green bell pepper, coarsely chopped

1 ripe avocado, chopped

2 scallions, chopped

1 jalapeño pepper, seeded (if desired) and chopped

1 clove garlic, chopped

1½ cups cubed ciabatta bread

¼ cup fresh basil, parsley *or* cilantro

¾ teaspoon salt

¼ teaspoon ground pepper

⅔ cup whole-milk plain yogurt

2 tablespoons extra-virgin olive oil

1 tablespoon white-wine vinegar

1-1½ cups low-sodium chicken broth

1. Combine tomatillos, tomatoes, cucumber, bell pepper, avocado, scallions, jalapeño, garlic, bread, basil (or parsley or cilantro), salt and pepper in a large bowl. Transfer half the mixture to a food processor. Puree until almost smooth, scraping down the sides once or twice. (If necessary, let the mixture rest for a few minutes to allow the bread to soften, then continue to puree until smooth.) Transfer to a large container. Repeat with the remaining vegetable mixture.

2. Add yogurt, oil, vinegar and 1 cup broth to the soup. Adjust the consistency with more broth as desired. Cover and chill for at least 1 hour or up to 24 hours.

➤➤ **MAKE AHEAD:** Refrigerate for up to 3 days.

SERVES 6: ABOUT 1 CUP EACH

Calories 184 | Fat 12g (sat 2g) | Cholesterol 4mg | Carbs 15g | Total sugars 5g (added 0g) | Protein 6g | Fiber 4g | Sodium 374mg | Potassium 494mg.
Nutrition bonus: Vitamin C (54% daily value).

CHEESE TOASTS 6 WAYS

Soup's ultimate partner? Cheese toast. Start with a slice of toasted baguette and get creative with the toppings. Here are some of our favorite combinations. Don't worry, plain grilled cheese, we still love you— we just want to see other toasts too.

< GOAT CHEESE (1½ TBSP) + ROSEMARY + HONEY (1 TSP)

PROSCIUTTO (½ SLICE) + ARUGULA + PECORINO CHEESE (1½ TBSP) >

RICOTTA (1½ TBSP) +
LEMON ZEST + PEPPER

NEUFCHÂTEL (1 TBSP) +
SMOKED SALMON
(½ OZ) + DILL

TOMATO (2 SLICES) +
CHEDDAR CHEESE
(1½ TBSP)

FIG JAM (1 TSP) +
BLUE CHEESE (1½ TBSP) +
TOASTED WALNUTS
(2 HALVES)

KINDERSOUPS

Creamy tomato soup paired with a grilled cheese sandwich is a classic kid meal, but it's not the only soup kids love. These soups offer spins on favorite foods of the small fry—such as cheeseburgers, mac & cheese and chicken enchiladas—as well as a few globally inspired bowls to expand and pique their growing palates.

CHICKEN POTPIE SOUP
WITH TATER TOT
TOPPING
P.96

CHICKEN POTPIE SOUP WITH TATER TOT TOPPING

This bubbling stew-like soup is a great way to use up leftover cooked chicken or turkey—and a perfect excuse to indulge in crispy, puffy tater tots. *(Photo: page 94.)*

3 cups frozen potato tots

2 tablespoons canola oil

2 tablespoons unsalted butter

1 cup chopped carrot

1 cup chopped parsnip

½ cup chopped celery

½ cup chopped onion

½ cup all-purpose flour

6 cups low-sodium chicken broth

3 cups diced cooked chicken *or* turkey

1 teaspoon garlic powder

1 teaspoon onion powder

1 teaspoon dried marjoram

½ teaspoon dried sage

1 cup frozen peas

½ cup half-and-half

3 tablespoons chopped fresh parsley

1. Preheat oven to 450°F. Coat a large baking sheet with cooking spray.

2. Place potato tots on the prepared baking sheet. Bake until golden and crispy, 20 to 25 minutes.

3. Meanwhile, heat oil and butter in a large pot over medium heat. Add carrot, parsnip, celery and onion. Cook, stirring occasionally, until the vegetables start to soften, about 5 minutes. Stir in flour and cook, stirring, for 1 minute. Stir in broth, chicken (or turkey), garlic powder, onion powder, marjoram and sage. Bring to a boil over medium-high heat, stirring occasionally. Reduce heat and simmer until thickened and bubbly, about 2 minutes. Remove from heat. Stir in peas and half-and-half.

4. Arrange the potato tots over the surface of the soup. Serve topped with parsley.

SERVES 6: 1½ CUPS EACH

Calories 460 | Fat 21g (sat 6g) | Cholesterol 77mg | Carbs 38g | Total sugars 6g (added 0g) | Protein 32g | Fiber 5g | Sodium 490mg | Potassium 854mg.
Nutrition bonus: Vitamin A (89% daily value) | Vitamin C (22% dv).

PLANTAIN SOUP (SOPA DE PLATANOS)

Plantains are a starchier, less-sweet cousin to the banana. They're the star ingredient in this Puerto Rican soup and also help to thicken it as the soup simmers. The flavors are simple so the quality of the broth you use is especially important.

3 green plantains, peeled (*see Tip*)

1 teaspoon extra-virgin olive oil

2 cloves garlic, minced

½ cup finely chopped fresh cilantro, divided

8 cups low-sodium chicken broth

1½ cups water

1 teaspoon salt

  Ground pepper to taste

8 teaspoons finely shredded Parmesan cheese

8 lime wedges

1. Shred plantains using the large holes of a box grater.

2. Heat oil in a large saucepan over medium heat. Add garlic and ¼ cup cilantro; cook, stirring, until the garlic is softened, 1 to 2 minutes. Add broth and water and bring to a boil. Stir in the shredded plantain and reduce heat to a simmer. Simmer until the plantain is tender and the soup is thickened, 25 to 30 minutes.

3. Stir in the remaining ¼ cup cilantro and season with salt and pepper. Sprinkle each serving with 1 teaspoon Parmesan and garnish with a lime wedge.

SERVES 8: ABOUT 1 CUP EACH

Calories 134 | Fat 3g (sat 1g) | Cholesterol 1mg | Carbs 25g | Total sugars 10g (added 0g) | Protein 6g | Fiber 2g | Sodium 396mg | Potassium 552mg.
Nutrition bonus: Vitamin C (21% daily value).

Plantains are usually sold underripe with green-yellow skin—just what you'll need for this recipe. Find them at large supermarkets or Latin markets. To peel an unripe plantain, slice off both ends and cut into 3-inch lengths. Using the tip of a paring knife, cut 4 lengthwise slits along each piece, Soak in ice water for 3 to 5 minutes to loosen the skin. Remove from the water and peel.

CHUNKY CHEESEBURGER SOUP

Traditional toppings add so much crunch and flavor to this creamy burger soup that you won't even miss the bun!

1 pound 90%-lean ground beef

1 cup chopped celery

½ cup diced onion

4 cups low-sodium beef broth

1 cup water

4 cups diced peeled potatoes

4 tablespoons (½ stick) unsalted butter

¼ cup all-purpose flour

1½ cups low-fat milk

1 6-ounce can no-salt-added tomato paste

2 tablespoons ketchup

2 tablespoons Dijon mustard

2 cups shredded Cheddar & American cheese blend

1 tablespoon chopped fresh parsley

Chopped tomatoes, onion and/or dill pickle relish for garnish

1. Cook beef in a large pot over medium-high heat, crumbling with a wooden spoon, until no longer pink, about 5 minutes. Add celery and onion; cook, stirring, until the vegetables are softened, about 3 minutes. Add broth, water and potatoes. Bring to a boil. Reduce heat to a simmer, partially cover and cook, stirring occasionally, until the potatoes are tender, about 15 minutes.

2. Meanwhile, melt butter in a medium saucepan over medium heat. Whisk in flour. Slowly add milk, stirring constantly, and cook until thickened, about 2 minutes. Whisk in tomato paste, ketchup and mustard.

3. Slowly whisk the milk mixture into the soup and bring to a boil. Reduce heat to a simmer and stir in cheese, a handful at a time. Cook just until the cheese is melted. Remove from heat and stir in parsley. Serve topped with tomatoes, onion and relish, if desired.

SERVES 8: 1½ CUPS EACH

Calories 405 | Fat 23g (sat 12g) | Cholesterol 82mg | Carbs 23g | Total sugars 8g (added 1g) | Protein 25g | Fiber 3g | Sodium 429mg | Potassium 964mg.
Nutrition bonus: Vitamin B$_{12}$ (33% daily value) | Calcium (29% dv) | Vitamins A & C (22% dv).

LOW-CALORIE • VEGETARIAN • GLUTEN-FREE

SWEET POTATO-PEANUT BISQUE

This rich vegetarian soup is inspired by the flavors of West African peanut soup. We've given it the added jolt of hot green chiles, but you can use mild if you prefer. For a variation, stir in your favorite greens and, if you like, try chopped peanuts and scallions for a different garnish.

2 large sweet potatoes (10-12 ounces each)

1 tablespoon canola oil

1 small yellow onion, chopped

1 large clove garlic, minced

3 cups reduced-sodium tomato-vegetable juice blend *or* tomato juice

1 4-ounce can diced green chiles, preferably hot, drained

2 teaspoons minced fresh ginger

1 teaspoon ground allspice

1 15-ounce can vegetable broth

½ cup smooth natural peanut butter

Freshly ground pepper to taste

Chopped fresh cilantro leaves for garnish

1. Prick sweet potatoes in several places with a fork. Microwave on High until just cooked through, 7 to 10 minutes. Set aside to cool.

2. Meanwhile, heat oil in a large saucepan over medium-high heat. Add onion and cook, stirring, until it just begins to brown, 2 to 4 minutes. Add garlic and cook, stirring, for 1 minute more. Stir in juice, green chiles, ginger and allspice. Adjust the heat so the mixture boils gently; cook for 10 minutes.

3. Meanwhile, peel the sweet potatoes and chop into bite-size pieces. Add half to the pot. Place the other half in a food processor or blender along with broth and peanut butter. Puree until completely smooth.

4. Add the puree to the pot and stir well to combine. Thin the bisque with water, if desired. Season with pepper. Heat until hot. Garnish with cilantro, if desired.

▸▸ **MAKE AHEAD:** Refrigerate for up to 3 days. Thin with water before reheating, if desired.

SERVES 5: ABOUT 1½ CUPS EACH

Calories 302 | Fat 16g (sat 2g) | Cholesterol 0mg | Carbs 29g | Total sugars 12g (added 0g) | Protein 9g | Fiber 6g | Sodium 490mg | Potassium 862mg.
Nutrition bonus: Vitamin A (294% daily value) | Vitamin C (103% dv).

CHICKEN SOUP WITH PASSATELLI

This chicken soup is usually a first course in the northern Italian regions of Romagna and Marche. Passatelli is pasta made with breadcrumbs. Traditionally the breadcrumbs to use in this recipe come from plain Italian white bread that is a day or two old, but whole-grain breadcrumbs are delicious as well.

8 cups low-sodium chicken broth

2 large carrots, chopped

1 stalk celery, chopped

2 cloves garlic, peeled and crushed

¼ teaspoon salt

1½ cups fresh breadcrumbs (*see Tip*)

⅔ cup grated Parmesan cheese, plus more for garnish

1 teaspoon freshly grated nutmeg

2 large eggs

1 cup chopped fresh parsley

1. Bring broth to a boil in a large pot. Add carrots, celery, garlic and salt. Reduce the heat to medium-low and simmer for 30 minutes.

2. Meanwhile, combine breadcrumbs, cheese and nutmeg in a mixing bowl. Make a well in the center and add eggs; mix until thoroughly combined. The dough should be damp but firm. If necessary, incorporate additional breadcrumbs or a few drops of water; if the dough is too wet or too dry it will crumble.

3. To form the passatelli, pinch off a piece of dough and roll it out between your palms or on the work surface into a rope about ¼ inch thick, then break it into ½-inch lengths. Continue forming the rest of the dough in the same manner.

4. Bring the broth back to a boil, add the passatelli and parsley and cook for 5 minutes. Serve topped with more Parmesan, if desired.

SERVES 6: 1⅓ CUPS EACH

Calories 202 | Fat 8g (sat 3g) | Cholesterol 70mg | Carbs 22g | Total sugars 3g (added 1g) | Protein 12g | Fiber 2g | Sodium 538mg | Potassium 478mg.
Nutrition bonus: Vitamin A (102% daily value) | Vitamin C (26% dv) | Calcium (20% dv).

To make fresh breadcrumbs: Trim crusts from bread. Tear the bread into pieces and process in a food processor until coarse crumbs form. Once slice of bread makes about ⅓ cup crumbs.

LOADED BAKED POTATO SOUP

Here's a soup recipe with the comforting flavor of fully loaded baked potatoes with bacon, Cheddar, sour cream and chives. To make a vegetarian version, omit the bacon and use "no-chicken" broth. Serve it with a green salad and crusty bread to clean up the bowl.

- 1 tablespoon canola oil
- 2 slices bacon, cut in half
- ½ cup chopped onion
- 1½ pounds medium russet potatoes (2-3), scrubbed and diced
- 4 cups low-sodium chicken broth
- ½ cup reduced-fat sour cream
- ½ cup shredded extra-sharp Cheddar cheese, divided
- ¼ teaspoon salt
- ¼ teaspoon ground pepper
- ¼ cup snipped chives *or* finely chopped scallion greens

1. Heat oil in a large saucepan over medium heat. Add bacon and cook, turning occasionally, until crisp, 4 to 5 minutes. Transfer to a paper-towel-lined plate to drain, leaving the oil and bacon drippings in the pan. Add onion to the pan and cook, stirring, until starting to soften, 2 to 3 minutes. Add potatoes and broth. Bring to a boil. Reduce heat to maintain a simmer and cook until the potatoes are tender, 12 to 15 minutes.

2. Using a slotted spoon, transfer about half the potatoes to a bowl and mash until almost smooth, but still a little chunky. Return the mashed potatoes to the pan along with sour cream, ¼ cup cheese, salt and pepper. Cook, stirring, until the cheese is melted and the soup is heated through, 1 to 2 minutes. Serve topped with crumbled bacon, the remaining ¼ cup cheese and chives (or scallion greens).

SERVES 4: 1¾ CUPS EACH

Calories 328 | Fat 15g (sat 6g) | Cholesterol 29mg | Carbs 37g | Total sugars 2g (added 0g) | Protein 14g | Fiber 3g | Sodium 400mg | Potassium 1,023mg. Nutrition bonus: Vitamin C (22% daily value).

Adding vinegar to the egg-poaching water helps the whites coagulate so they take on a nice, tidy shape.

GREEN EGGS *AND* HAM SOUP

Would you, could you eat this creamy green soup? How about if we told you it contains no cream—or dairy of any kind—just flavorful pureed veggies topped with a perfectly poached egg and ham? Trust us, whether you eat it in a box or with a fox, in a house or with a mouse, both you and your kids will love this storybook-perfect soup.

2 tablespoons extra-virgin olive oil, divided

4 ounces thick-cut ham *or* prosciutto, diced

1 small onion, chopped

2 cloves garlic, minced

4 cups low-sodium chicken broth

4 cups chopped broccoli florets

2 cups chopped cauliflower florets

2 teaspoons fresh thyme

⅛ teaspoon salt

4 cups baby spinach

¼ cup chopped fresh parsley, plus more for garnish

8 cups water

2 tablespoons distilled white vinegar

4 large eggs

1. Heat 1 tablespoon oil in a large pot over medium heat. Add ham (or prosciutto) and cook, stirring often, until lightly browned, about 3 minutes. Transfer to a plate and set aside.

2. Add the remaining 1 tablespoon oil and onion to the pot. Cook, stirring often, until softened, about 3 minutes. Add garlic; cook, stirring, for 1 minute. Add broth, broccoli, cauliflower, thyme and salt. Reduce heat to a simmer, cover and cook until the broccoli is very tender, about 6 minutes. Add spinach and parsley. Remove from heat and let stand, covered, until the spinach is wilted, about 5 minutes. Puree the soup in the pot with an immersion blender or in batches in a regular blender. (Use caution when blending hot liquids.) Cover to keep warm.

3. Meanwhile, bring water and vinegar to a boil in a large saucepan. Reduce to a bare simmer. Gently stir in a circle so the water is swirling around the pan. Break an egg into a small bowl, then submerge the lip of the bowl into the simmering water and gently add the egg. Working quickly, repeat with remaining eggs. Cook for 4 minutes for soft set, 5 minutes for medium set and 8 minutes for hard set.

4. Serve the soup topped with a poached egg, some ham (or prosciutto) and parsley, if desired.

SERVES 4: 1½ CUPS EACH

Calories 266 | Fat 15g (sat 4g) | Cholesterol 199mg | Carbs 14g | Total sugars 3g (added 0g) | Protein 22g | Fiber 5g | Sodium 671mg | Potassium 818mg. Nutrition bonus: Vitamin C (208% daily value) | Vitamin A (128% dv) | Folate (55% dv) | Iron (26% dv).

SQUISH-SQUASH MAC *and* CHEESE SOUP

A package of pureed cooked winter squash adds a touch of sweetness and good nutrition—namely vitamin A, potassium and fiber—to this family-pleasing soup. Feel free to swap in your favorite shape of medium-size pasta for the elbow macaroni.

1½ cups whole-wheat elbow macaroni
3 tablespoons unsalted butter
3 tablespoons all-purpose flour
2 teaspoons Dijon mustard
4 cups low-sodium chicken broth
1 10-ounce box frozen pureed winter squash, thawed slightly
2 cups half-and-half
1 8-ounce package reduced-fat cream cheese, cubed and softened
1½ cups shredded Cheddar cheese
2 teaspoons cornstarch
2 teaspoons white-wine vinegar
½ teaspoon salt
¼ teaspoon ground pepper
Sliced chives for garnish

1. Cook macaroni according to package directions. Drain and set aside.

2. Meanwhile, melt butter in a large pot over medium heat. Add flour and mustard and whisk for 2 minutes. Gradually add broth, stirring constantly. Bring to a boil.

3. Add squash and return to a boil. Stir in half-and-half and bring to a simmer. Add cream cheese, whisking constantly until it is melted. Remove from heat.

4. Combine shredded cheese and cornstarch in a medium bowl, tossing to coat evenly. Slowly add the cheese to the soup, stirring constantly until melted. Stir in the macaroni, vinegar, salt and pepper. Top with chives, if desired.

SERVES 8: 1¼ CUPS EACH

Calories 381 | Fat 26g (sat 15g) | Cholesterol 74mg | Carbs 25g | Total sugars 4g (added 0g) | Protein 15g | Fiber 2g | Sodium 478mg | Potassium 357mg.
Nutrition bonus: Vitamin A (142% daily value) | Calcium (27% dv).

CREAMY TOMATO SOUP WITH TORTELLINI

Luscious, slightly sweet and studded with cheese-filled pasta pillows, this tomato soup is a dream bowl for kids. Make sure to save some for them.

1 tablespoon extra-virgin olive oil

1 tablespoon butter

1 large leek, white & light green parts only, halved lengthwise, rinsed and sliced *(see Tip, page 197)*

4 cloves garlic, minced

1 6-ounce can no-salt-added tomato paste

4 cups low-sodium vegetable broth *or* "no-chicken" broth *(see page 224)*

1 28-ounce can Italian plum tomatoes, drained and chopped

2 bay leaves

1 teaspoon crushed dried oregano *(see Tip)*

1 teaspoon salt

1 9-ounce package cheese tortellini, fresh *or* frozen

1 tablespoon all-purpose flour

1½ cups half-and-half

½ cup chopped fresh basil *or* parsley

1. Heat oil and butter in a large pot over medium heat. Add leek and garlic. Cook, stirring often, until softened, 2 to 3 minutes. Stir in tomato paste. Cook, stirring, for 2 minutes. Add broth, tomatoes, bay leaves, oregano and salt. Bring to a boil, stirring occasionally. Reduce heat and simmer for 10 minutes.

2. Add tortellini. Simmer until the tortellini are tender, 4 to 7 minutes.

3. Remove the bay leaves. Whisk flour and half-and-half in a small bowl. Stir the mixture into the soup. Add basil (or parsley). Cook, stirring occasionally, until slightly thickened, about 1 minute.

SERVES 6: 1½ CUPS EACH

Calories 322 | Fat 14g (sat 7g) | Cholesterol 44mg | Carbs 40g | Total sugars 12g (added 0g) | Protein 11g | Fiber 4g | Sodium 520mg | Potassium 476mg. Nutrition bonus: Vitamin A (28% daily value).

To crush dried herbs, press and rub them in your hand. This releases their aromatic, flavor-infusing oils before you cook with them.

CHICKEN ENCHILADA SOUP

Queso meets enchilada in this rich and cheesy Mexican-style soup. Serve it with something fresh, light and crunchy—like a jicama slaw dressed in a little olive oil, lime juice, salt, and pepper.

1 tablespoon canola oil

1 cup chopped onion

3 cloves garlic, minced

5 cups low-sodium chicken broth

1 15-ounce can diced tomatoes

1 4-ounce can diced green chiles

6 corn tortillas, chopped

2 teaspoons chili powder

1 teaspoon ground cumin

2 cups shredded cooked chicken breast

4 ounces reduced-fat cream cheese, softened

¾ cup shredded white Cheddar cheese

1½ teaspoons cornstarch

Fresh cilantro, sour cream *and/or* guacamole for garnish

1. Heat oil in a large pot over medium heat. Add onion and cook, stirring occasionally, until soft but not browned, about 3 minutes. Add garlic and cook, stirring, for 1 minute. Add broth, tomatoes, chiles, tortillas, chili powder and cumin. Bring to a boil, stirring occasionally. Reduce heat to a simmer. Cover and cook for 20 minutes.

2. Add chicken and cream cheese, stirring until the cream cheese is melted. Remove from heat. Combine shredded cheese and cornstarch in a small bowl and gradually add to the soup, stirring until melted. Return the pot to medium heat and cook until hot, 1 to 2 minutes. Serve the soup with cilantro, sour cream and/or guacamole, if desired.

SERVES 6: 1½ CUPS EACH

Calories 395 | Fat 21g (sat 10g) | Cholesterol 86mg | Carbs 24g | Total sugars 6g (added 0g) | Protein 29g | Fiber 3g | Sodium 561mg | Potassium 470mg.
Nutrition bonus: Calcium (26% daily value) | Vitamin C (22% dv).

CHICKEN CURRY ZOODLE SOUP

SPICY RAMEN WITH MUSHROOMS *and* SPINACH

SHRIMP *and* KIMCHI NOODLE SOUP

FAUX CHICKEN PHO

MISO SOUP WITH SHRIMP *and* GREEN TEA SOBA

SICHUAN RAMEN WITH CABBAGE *and* TOFU

Make your own cups of instant soup with these fresh and flavorful recipes. Pack several jars at once for lunch throughout the week!

JUST ADD WATER

COCONUT CURRY WITH
BUTTERNUT SQUASH NOODLES

SHRIMP *and* KIMCHI
NOODLE SOUP
P.118

SPICY RAMEN WITH
MUSHROOMS *and* SPINACH
P.119

CHICKEN CURRY
ZOODLE SOUP
P.120

SICHUAN RAMEN
WITH CABBAGE *and* TOFU
P.124

COCONUT CURRY
WITH BUTTERNUT
SQUASH NOODLES
P.123

MISO SOUP WITH
SHRIMP AND GREEN
TEA SOBA
P.122

FAUX
CHICKEN PHO
P.121

SHRIMP *AND* KIMCHI NOODLE SOUP

Ubiquitous in Korean cuisine, kimchi adds heat and a little funk to this DIY soup-to-go. Look for it near other refrigerated fermented vegetables. *(Photos: pages 114 & 116.)*

EQUIPMENT: THREE 1½-PINT WIDE-MOUTH CANNING JARS

- 3 teaspoons reduced-sodium chicken bouillon paste *(see page 224)*
- 3 teaspoons gochujang (Korean chile paste) *or* chile-garlic sauce
- 1½ cups chopped cabbage
- 1½ cups sliced mushrooms
- ¾ cup chopped kimchi
- 9 ounces peeled cooked shrimp
- 1½ cups cooked rice noodles *(see Tip)*
- 1 radish, thinly sliced
- 3 teaspoons chopped fresh cilantro
- 3 lime wedges
- 3 cups very hot water, divided

1. Add 1 teaspoon each bouillon paste and gochujang to each of three 1½-pint canning jars. Layer ½ cup each cabbage and mushrooms, ¼ cup kimchi, 3 ounces shrimp and ½ cup noodles into each jar. Top each with some radish slices, 1 teaspoon cilantro and a lime wedge. Cover and refrigerate.

2. To prepare each jar: Squeeze the lime into the jar (discard the wedge). Add 1 cup very hot water to a jar, cover and shake until the seasonings are dissolved. Uncover and microwave on High in 1-minute increments until steaming hot, 2 to 3 minutes total. Stir well. Let stand a few minutes before eating.

➤ **MAKE AHEAD:** Prepare through Step 1. Refrigerate covered jars for up to 3 days.

SERVES 3: 2 CUPS EACH

Calories 239 | Fat 1g (sat 0g) | Cholesterol 161mg | Carbs 32g | Total sugars 5g (added 1g) | Protein 26g | Fiber 3g | Sodium 926mg | Potassium 408mg. Nutrition bonus: Vitamin C (26% daily value).

For 1½ cups cooked noodles, start with 3 to 4 ounces. Boil the noodles about 1 minute less than the package directions so they are slightly underdone. Drain and rinse well with cold water before assembling jars.

SPICY RAMEN WITH MUSHROOMS *AND* SPINACH

Chinese chile-garlic sauce is a double-duty ingredient in this vegetarian ramen-in-a-jar, adding a touch of spicy heat and garlicky flavor too. Look for this blend of ground chiles, garlic and vinegar in the Asian section of large supermarkets. *(Photos: pages 114 & 116.)*

EQUIPMENT: THREE 1½-PINT WIDE-MOUTH CANNING JARS

- 1½ tablespoons reduced-sodium vegetable bouillon paste *(see page 224)*
- 1½ teaspoons white miso *(see Tip, page 149)*
- 1½ teaspoons chile-garlic sauce
- 1½ teaspoons grated fresh ginger
- ¾ cup shredded carrot
- ¾ cup sliced shiitake mushroom caps (about 1½ ounces)
- 1½ cups chopped baby spinach
- 3 hard-boiled eggs, peeled and halved *(see Tip, page 123)*
- 1½ cups cooked ramen noodles *(see Tip, page 118)*
- 3 tablespoons sliced scallions
- ¾ teaspoon toasted sesame seeds
- 3 cups very hot water, divided

1. Add ½ tablespoon bouillon paste and ½ teaspoon each miso, chile-garlic sauce and ginger to each of three 1½-pint canning jars. Layer ¼ cup each carrot and mushrooms, ½ cup spinach, 2 egg halves and ½ cup noodles into each jar. Top each with 1 tablespoon scallions and ¼ teaspoon sesame seeds. Cover and refrigerate.

2. To prepare each jar: Add 1 cup very hot water to a jar, cover and shake until the seasonings are dissolved. Uncover and microwave on High in 1-minute increments until steaming hot, 2 to 3 minutes. Stir to make sure the miso is dissolved. Let stand a few minutes before eating.

➤➤ **MAKE AHEAD:** Prepare through Step 1. Refrigerate covered jars for up to 3 days.

SERVES 3: 2 CUPS EACH

Calories 366 | Fat 7g (sat 2g) | Cholesterol 240mg | Carbs 64g | Total sugars 2g (added 0g) | Protein 16g | Fiber 12g | Sodium 866mg | Potassium 219mg. Nutrition bonus: Vitamin A (135% daily value) | Iron (26% dv) | Folate (22% dv).

CHICKEN CURRY ZOODLE SOUP

Look for premade zucchini noodles at most large supermarkets and natural-foods stores or spiralize one small zucchini to make this recipe. You can tailor this soup to your taste by using different kinds of curry paste, such as yellow, green or massaman style. *(Photos: pages 114 & 116.)*

EQUIPMENT: THREE 1½-PINT WIDE-MOUTH CANNING JARS

- 6 tablespoons coconut milk
- 6 teaspoons Thai red curry paste (*see Tip*)
- 3 teaspoons reduced-sodium chicken bouillon paste (*see page 224*)
- 1½ cups frozen stir-fry vegetable mix
- 9 ounces chopped cooked chicken breast (about 2¼ cups)
- 1½ cups spiralized zucchini noodles
- 3 teaspoons chopped fresh cilantro
- 3 cups very hot water, divided

1. Add 2 tablespoons coconut milk, 2 teaspoons curry paste and 1 teaspoon bouillon paste to each of three 1½-pint canning jars. Layer ½ cup vegetables, 3 ounces chicken (about ¾ cup) and ½ cup noodles into each jar. Top each with 1 teaspoon cilantro. Cover and refrigerate.

2. To prepare each jar: Add 1 cup very hot water to a jar, cover and shake until the seasonings are dissolved. Uncover and microwave on High in 1-minute increments until steaming hot, 2 to 3 minutes total. Stir well. Let stand a few minutes before eating.

▸▸ **MAKE AHEAD:** Prepare through Step 1. Refrigerate covered jars for up to 3 days.

SERVES 3: 2 CUPS EACH

Calories 235 | Fat 8g (sat 5g) | Cholesterol 72mg | Carbs 9g | Total sugars 5g (added 0g) | Protein 29g | Fiber 1g | Sodium 825mg | Potassium 324mg.
Nutrition bonus: Vitamin C (25% daily value).

Look for red or green Thai curry paste, a mixture of chiles and Thai seasonings, in the Asian section of large supermarkets. The heat and salt level can vary widely depending on brand.

FAUX CHICKEN PHO

Grating ginger and garlic with a microplane transforms them into a paste that easily mixes into the broth in this almost-instant pho. Don't have cooked chicken? Thinly sliced cooked steak, shrimp or cubed tofu are tasty alternatives. *(Photos: pages 114 & 117.)*

EQUIPMENT: THREE 1½-PINT WIDE-MOUTH
                CANNING JARS

- 3 teaspoons reduced-sodium chicken bouillon paste *(see page 224)*
- 1½ teaspoons grated fresh ginger
- 1½ teaspoons grated garlic
- 1½ teaspoons hoisin sauce
- 1½ teaspoons Sriracha
- ¾ teaspoon fish sauce
- 3 whole star anise
- ½ jalapeño pepper, seeded (if desired) and thinly sliced
- 1½ heaping cups sliced shiitake mushroom caps (about 3 ounces)
- 9 ounces shredded cooked chicken (about 2¼ cups)
- 1½ cups cooked wide brown rice noodles *(see Tip, page 118)*
- 3 tablespoons thinly sliced scallions
- 3 lime wedges
- ¾ cup bean sprouts
- 3 tablespoons small mint leaves
- 3 tablespoons small basil leaves
- 3 cups very hot water, divided

1. Add 1 teaspoon bouillon paste, ½ teaspoon each ginger, garlic, hoisin and Sriracha, ¼ teaspoon fish sauce, 1 star anise and one-third of the jalapeño slices to each of three 1½-pint canning jars. Layer ½ cup mushrooms, 3 ounces chicken (about ¾ cup) and ½ cup noodles into each jar. Top each with 1 tablespoon scallions, 1 lime wedge, ¼ cup sprouts and 1 tablespoon each mint and basil. Cover and refrigerate.

2. To prepare each jar: Remove the bean sprouts and herbs (don't worry about getting every last bit out). Squeeze the lime into the jar (discard the wedge). Add 1 cup very hot water, cover and shake until the seasonings are dissolved. Uncover and microwave on High in 1-minute increments until steaming hot, 2 to 3 minutes. Let stand for a minute or two, then stir well. Discard the star anise. Return the bean sprouts and herbs to the jar before eating.

▸ **MAKE AHEAD:** Prepare through Step 1. Refrigerate covered jars for up to 3 days.

SERVES 3: 2½ CUPS EACH

Calories 395 | Fat 5g (sat 1g) | Cholesterol 72mg | Carbs 54g | Total sugars 5g (added 1g) | Protein 34g | Fiber 6g | Sodium 760mg | Potassium 419mg.
Nutrition bonus: Vitamin C (22% daily value).

ACTIVE 25 MIN
TOTAL 25 MIN

LOW-CALORIE

MISO SOUP WITH SHRIMP AND GREEN TEA SOBA

Green tea soba noodles, or cha soba, are buckwheat noodles made with powdered green tea, which imparts a subtle grassy note and pretty color. You can find them in many large supermarkets, Japanese markets or online. Or just use regular buckwheat soba noodles. Seaweeds and kelp, such as kombu and wakame, add essential umami to the broth. Find them in natural-foods stores and Asian markets. (Photos: pages 114 & 117.)

EQUIPMENT: THREE 1½-PINT WIDE-MOUTH CANNING JARS

- 4 tablespoons white miso (see Tip, page 149)
- 6 teaspoons mirin
- 3 teaspoons unseasoned rice vinegar
- 1½ cups diagonally sliced snow peas (about 5 ounces)
- 9 ounces peeled cooked shrimp
- 1½ teaspoons dried wakame
- 1½ cups cooked green tea soba noodles (see Tip, page 118)
- 3 tablespoons thinly sliced scallions
- 1 3-inch square dried kombu, snipped into 3 equal strips
- 3 cups very hot water, divided

1. Add 1 tablespoon plus 1 teaspoon miso, 2 teaspoons mirin and 1 teaspoon vinegar to each of three 1½-pint canning jars. Layer ½ cup snow peas, 3 ounces shrimp, ½ teaspoon wakame and ½ cup noodles into each jar. Top each with 1 table-spoon scallions. Fit 1 piece of kombu between the ingredients and the side of each jar. Cover and refrigerate.

2. To prepare each jar: Add 1 cup very hot water to the jar, cover and shake very well to dissolve the miso. Uncover and microwave on High in 1-minute increments until steaming hot, 2 to 3 minutes total. Discard the kombu. Stir to make sure the miso is dissolved. Let stand a few minutes before eating.

▸▸ **MAKE AHEAD:** Prepare through Step 1. Refrigerate covered jars for up to 3 days.

SERVES 3: 2 CUPS EACH

Calories 230 | Fat 1g (sat 0g) | Cholesterol 161mg | Carbs 30g | Total sugars 9g (added 1g) | Protein 27g | Fiber 2g | Sodium 789mg | Potassium 361mg. Nutrition bonus: Vitamin C (41% daily value).

COCONUT CURRY WITH BUTTERNUT SQUASH NOODLES

This unconventional spin on Thai red curry features spiralized butternut squash noodles, but you could also use spiralized sweet potatoes or fresh egg noodles. *(Photos: pages 115 & 117.)*

EQUIPMENT: THREE 1½-PINT WIDE-MOUTH CANNING JARS

- 6 **tablespoons coconut milk**
- 6 **teaspoons Thai red curry paste** (*see Tip, page 120*)
- 3 **teaspoons fish sauce**
- 1½ **teaspoons packed light brown sugar**
- 2¼ **cups thinly sliced bok choy (about 5 ounces)**
- 3 **cups lightly packed spiralized butternut squash noodles**
- 3 **tablespoons toasted unsweetened coconut chips**
- 3 **lime wedges**
- 3 **medium-boiled eggs (*see Tip*), peeled**
- 3 **cups very hot water, divided**

1. Add 2 tablespoons coconut milk, 2 teaspoons curry paste, 1 teaspoon fish sauce and ½ teaspoon brown sugar to each of three 1½-pint canning jars. Layer ¾ cup bok choy and 1 cup noodles into each jar. Top each with 1 tablespoon coconut, 1 lime wedge and 1 egg. Cover and refrigerate.

2. To prepare each jar: Remove the egg. Squeeze the lime into the jar (discard the wedge). Add 1 cup very hot water, cover and shake until the seasonings are dissolved. Uncover and microwave on High in 1-minute increments until steaming hot, 3 to 4 minutes. Stir well. Cut the egg in half and return it to the jar. Let stand a few minutes before eating.

▸▸ **MAKE AHEAD:** Prepare through Step 1. Refrigerate covered jars for up to 3 days.

SERVES 3: 2 CUPS EACH

Calories 217 | Fat 13g (sat 9g) | Cholesterol 164mg | Carbs 18g | Total sugars 6g (added 2g) | Protein 9g | Fiber 3g | Sodium 734mg | Potassium 561mg. Nutrition bonus: Vitamin A (232% daily value) | Vitamin C (72% dv) | Folate (20% dv).

For medium-boiled eggs with jammy-textured yolks, cook in simmering water for 6½ to 7 minutes, then immediately transfer to a bowl of ice water and let stand until cold. For fully cooked hard-boiled eggs, cook in boiling water for 10 minutes before transferring them to the ice bath.

SICHUAN RAMEN WITH CABBAGE *AND* TOFU

Sichuan Province in the southwestern corner of China is known for its fiery dishes. Here, the richness of tahini tempers the spicy chile paste and brings a familiar sesame oil-like flavor to the soup. Sichuan peppercorns add a pleasantly mouth-numbing heat that's also a calling card for dishes from this region. Buy them at Asian markets or online. There's no great substitute for these peppercorns, but if you can't find them, try making this with the same amount of Chinese five-spice powder instead. *(Photos: pages 114 & 116.)*

EQUIPMENT: THREE 1½-PINT WIDE-MOUTH CANNING JARS

- 6 teaspoons Sichuan chile-bean sauce *(toban djan)* **or** chile-garlic sauce
- 6 teaspoons tahini
- 1½ teaspoons reduced-sodium vegetable bouillon paste *(see page 224)*
- 1½ teaspoons Chinese rice wine
- 1½ teaspoons packed light brown sugar
- ¾ teaspoon black vinegar *(see Tip)*
- 3 cups shredded napa cabbage
- 9 ounces extra-firm tofu, cut into ½-inch cubes (about 1½ heaping cups)
- ¾ teaspoons Sichuan peppercorns, coarsely ground
- 1½ cups cooked black **or** brown rice ramen noodles *(see Tip, page 118)*
- 1½ teaspoons toasted sesame seeds
- 3 cups very hot water, divided

1. Add 2 teaspoons each chile-bean sauce (or chile-garlic sauce) and tahini, ½ teaspoon each bouillon paste, rice wine and brown sugar and ¼ teaspoon vinegar to each of three 1½-pint canning jars. Layer 1 cup cabbage, 3 ounces tofu (about ½ cup), ¼ teaspoon ground peppercorns and ½ cup ramen noodles into each jar. Top each with ½ teaspoon sesame seeds. Cover and refrigerate.

2. To prepare each jar: Add 1 cup very hot water to the jar, cover and shake until the seasonings are dissolved. Uncover and microwave on High in 1-minute increments until steaming hot, 2 to 3 minutes. Stir well. Let stand a few minutes before eating.

▶▶ **MAKE AHEAD:** Prepare through Step 1. Refrigerate covered jars for up to 3 days.

SERVES 3: 2 CUPS EACH

Calories 396 | Fat 12g (sat 2g) | Cholesterol 50mg | Carbs 61g | Total sugars 3g (added 2g) | Protein 19g | Fiber 11g | Sodium 578mg | Potassium 337mg. Nutrition bonus: Calcium & Iron (29% daily value) | Vitamin C (20% dv).

Black vinegar—or ching-kiang vinegar—adds a rich, smoky flavor to many Chinese dishes. Look for it in Asian markets and specialty food shops. Balsamic, sherry or white vinegars can be used as substitutes.

MORE CUP-OF-NOODLES

Love making your own cup-of-noodles after trying these recipes?
Here's how to get started creating new combos.

START WITH THE RIGHT EQUIPMENT

You'll need three 1½-pint wide-mouth canning jars to make these soups. Why three? Because each soup keeps for three days in your fridge. Eat all the jars yourself, send them to work or school with your family or adjust the recipe to make fewer—or more. Pick wide-mouth jars because they make it easier to layer in ingredients.

LAYER YOUR CHOICE OF INGREDIENTS

PICK A FLAVOR BASE: Choose one or several and use 1 to 3 tablespoons total per serving:

- Bouillon or stock base
- Chile-garlic sauce
- Chipotles in adobo sauce
- Citrus juices (lemon, lime, orange)
- Coconut milk
- Curry paste
- Harissa
- Mirin
- Miso
- Peanut satay sauce
- Pesto
- Tahini
- Tomato paste
- Vinegar
- Yuzukosho

CHOOSE YOUR NOODLES: ½ cup cooked noodles or spiralized raw vegetable noodles per serving:

- Beet noodles
- Butternut squash noodles
- Ramen noodles
- Rice noodles
- Shirataki noodles
- Soba noodles
- Udon noodles
- Whole-wheat noodles
- Zucchini noodles

ADD VEGETABLES: For each serving use ½ to 1 cup of quick-cooking vegetables or at least cut the vegetables so they'll cook up fast.

- Broccoli
- Cabbage
- Carrots, shredded
- Collards
- Corn
- Edamame
- Green beans
- Greens
- Kale
- Mushrooms
- Peppers
- Radishes, sliced
- Shoots
- Frozen vegetables

ADD SOME PROTEIN: 3 ounces tofu or cooked meat, poultry, seafood or beans per serving:

- Canned beans
- Chicken
- Duck
- Hard-boiled eggs
- Pork
- Salmon
- Shrimp
- Steak
- Tempeh
- Tofu
- Turkey

FINISHING TOUCHES: Add these for flavor and flair:

- Chile flakes
- Chinese five-spice powder
- Fresh herbs
- Lime or lemon wedges
- Scallions
- Toasted sesame seeds
- Minced shallot
- Shichimi togarashi (Japanese seven-spice powder)
- Spice blends (Italian seasoning, garam masala)

TO PREPARE EACH JAR

Add 1 cup very hot water to the jar, cover and shake very well. Uncover and microwave on High in 1-minute increments until steaming hot, 2 to 3 minutes total. Stir and then let stand a few minutes before eating.

CUBAN BLACK BEAN SOUP
P.134

BEANS, BEANS

Cheap, tasty and incredibly versatile, legumes pack a soup with protein and fiber. And research actually backs up what that children's rhyme says: they really are good for your heart. These satisfying soups use both canned and dried beans, span from lentils to limas, and draw on a world of flavors for inspiration. If you think you're not a bean lover, these soups will change your mind.

LOW-CALORIE • GLUTEN-FREE

WHITE BEAN *and* VEGETABLE SOUP

Using dried beans gives this soup more complex flavor. This is a great recipe to double so you'll have leftovers to freeze for later.

1 cup dried cannellini beans, soaked for 8 hours *or* overnight

1 tablespoon extra-virgin olive oil

2 leeks, trimmed, washed and chopped *(see Tip, page 197)*

2 carrots, peeled and diced

1 clove garlic, finely chopped

6 plum tomatoes, seeded and chopped, or one 14-ounce can plum tomatoes, drained, seeded and coarsely chopped

6 new potatoes, peeled and diced

8 cups low-sodium chicken broth

¾ cup dry white wine

1 sprig fresh thyme *or* 1 teaspoon dried thyme

1 sprig fresh rosemary *or* 1 teaspoon dried rosemary

1 bay leaf

¾ teaspoon salt

1. Drain and rinse beans.

2. Heat oil in a large pot over medium-low heat. Add leeks, carrots and garlic; cook until softened, about 5 minutes. Stir in tomatoes and cook for 5 minutes. Add potatoes and cook for 5 minutes. Add broth, wine, thyme, rosemary and bay leaf; bring to a boil. Add the beans to the pot; cook until the beans are soft, 45 minutes to 2 hours. (Bean-cooking times can vary widely.)

3. To serve, remove the bay leaf and herb sprigs; season with salt.

▸▸ **MAKE AHEAD:** Refrigerate for up to 3 days or freeze for up to 3 months.

SERVES 6: GENEROUS 1 CUP EACH

Calories 288 | Fat 5g (sat 1g) | Cholesterol 0mg | Carbs 44g | Total sugars 7g (added 0g) | Protein 16g | Fiber 10g | Sodium 432mg | Potassium 908mg.
Nutrition bonus: Vitamin A (88% daily value) | Vitamin C (33 % dv).

BEAN AND BARLEY SOUP

This hearty soup tastes like it has simmered for hours, but actually it's quite quick to put together. If you have cooked barley on hand, omit the quick barley and stir in 1½ cups cooked barley along with the spinach in Step 2.

- 4 teaspoons extra-virgin olive oil
- 1 large onion, chopped
- 1 medium fennel bulb, cored and chopped
- 5 cloves garlic, minced
- 1 teaspoon dried basil
- 1 15-ounce can cannellini *or* other white beans, rinsed
- 1 14-ounce can fire-roasted diced tomatoes
- 6 cups low-sodium vegetable broth
- ¾ cup quick barley
- 1 5-ounce package baby spinach (6 cups)
- ¼ cup grated Parmesan cheese, plus more for serving
- ¼ teaspoon ground pepper

1. Heat oil in a large pot over medium-high heat. Add onion, fennel, garlic and basil; cook, stirring frequently, until the vegetables are tender and just beginning to brown, 6 to 8 minutes.

2. Mash ½ cup of beans. Stir the mashed and whole beans, tomatoes, broth and barley into the pot. Bring to a boil over high heat. Reduce heat to medium and simmer, stirring occasionally, until the barley is tender, about 15 minutes. Stir in spinach and cook until wilted, about 1 minute. Remove from heat and stir in cheese and pepper. Serve topped with more cheese, if desired.

▸▸ **MAKE AHEAD:** Refrigerate for up to 3 days or freeze for up to 6 months.

SERVES 4: 2½ CUPS EACH

Calories 333 | Fat 8g (sat 2g) | Cholesterol 4mg | Carbs 55g | Total sugars 11g (added 0g) | Protein 13g | Fiber 12g | Sodium 619mg | Potassium 832mg.
Nutrition bonus: Vitamin C (62% daily value) | Vitamin A (38% dv) | Folate (25% dv).

SPRING LIMA BEAN SOUP WITH CRISPY BACON

Not a lima bean lover? This soup could flip you. The limas get some support from baby peas and a decent amount of tarragon to deliver a definitive taste of spring.

 4 strips bacon, chopped

 1 tablespoon extra-virgin olive oil,
    plus more for serving

1½ cups diced onions

 1 cup thinly sliced celery

 2 cloves garlic, minced

6½ cups water

 1 pound Yukon Gold potatoes, diced

 1 teaspoon salt

½ teaspoon ground pepper

 2 16-ounce bags frozen baby lima beans

 1 cup frozen peas

¼ cup chopped fresh tarragon

 2 tablespoons chopped fresh parsley

 2 teaspoons white-wine vinegar

1. Cook bacon in a large pot over medium heat until browned and crisp, about 5 minutes. Use a slotted spoon to transfer to a paper-towel-lined plate.

2. Drain off all but 1 tablespoon bacon fat. Add oil, onions and celery and cook over medium heat, stirring occasionally, until soft, about 5 minutes. Add garlic and cook, stirring frequently, for 30 seconds. Add water, potatoes, salt and pepper. Bring to a boil. Reduce heat to a simmer, cover and cook until the potatoes are tender, 8 to 10 minutes.

3. Add lima beans and peas. Return to a boil over high heat and cook, uncovered, for 3 minutes. Remove from heat. Stir in tarragon, parsley and vinegar. Serve topped with bacon and a drizzle of oil, if desired.

SERVES 8: 1½ CUPS EACH

Calories 270 | Fat 5g (sat 1g) | Cholesterol 5mg | Carbs 45g | Total sugars 3g (added 0g) | Protein 12g | Fiber 9g | Sodium 460mg | Potassium 672mg.
Nutrition bonus: Vitamin A (31% daily value) | Iron (20% dv).

CUBAN BLACK BEAN SOUP

Unlike many black bean soups, this one is pepper-packed and leaves the beans intact for a more interesting texture. It's equally delicious served on its own or over rice. *(Photo: page 126.)*

2½ cups dry black beans, soaked for 8 hours *or* overnight

2 medium yellow onions, divided

2 medium green bell peppers, divided

1 smoked ham hock (1¼ pounds)

2 bay leaves

8 cups water

2 tablespoons extra-virgin olive oil

4 cloves garlic, minced

1 Cubanelle *or* jalapeño pepper (*see Tip*), seeded and finely chopped

1 teaspoon ground cumin

1 teaspoon dried oregano

¾ teaspoon salt

1 tablespoon white-wine vinegar *or* cider vinegar

Sliced roasted red peppers, jalapeño, avocado, red onion & lime wedges for garnish

1. Drain and rinse beans. Finely chop 1 onion and half of the second and set aside. Finely chop 1 bell pepper and set aside. Cut the other into quarters.

2. Combine the beans, the remaining half onion, the quartered bell pepper, ham hock, bay leaves and water in a pot. Bring to a boil over high heat. Reduce heat to a simmer, cover and cook until the beans are tender, about 1½ hours.

3. Transfer the ham hock to a clean cutting board and let cool. Discard the onion, bell pepper and bay leaves. Transfer 1 cup of the beans to a small bowl and mash with a fork. Remove the meat from the ham hock and chop.

4. Heat oil in a large skillet over medium-high heat. Add garlic and cook until fragrant, about 30 seconds. Add Cubanelle (or jalapeño) and the reserved chopped onions and bell pepper. Cook, stirring occasionally, until the vegetables are tender, about 4 minutes. Add cumin, oregano and salt; cook, stirring, for 1 minute. Add vinegar, scraping up any browned bits. Add the mashed beans and cook for 1 minute.

5. Add the vegetables and ham to the beans in the pot. Heat over medium heat, stirring, until hot, about 5 minutes. Serve topped with roasted red peppers, jalapeño, avocado, red onion and lime wedges, if desired.

SERVES 8: 1¼ CUPS EACH

Calories 310 | Fat 6g (sat 1g) | Cholesterol 21mg | Carbs 41g | Total sugars 3g (added 0g) | Protein 23g | Fiber 10g | Sodium 887mg | Potassium 1,119mg.
Nutrition bonus: Folate (69% daily value) | Vitamin C (52% dv) | Iron (21% dv).

Also called Cuban peppers or Italian frying peppers, Cubanelle peppers are long, slender and light yellow-green when unripe—which is how they are usually sold (they turn red when allowed to ripen). They have mild to very moderate heat and a rich, fruity flavor.

SOUP BEANS

Like poor people everywhere, mountain dwellers in the South thrived for centuries on food that was indigenous, inexpensive and healthful. These days "soup beans" speak homey comfort to anyone who has familial connections to Appalachia, where every garden produced shelling beans that could be eaten fresh or grown to maturity for dry beans. Serve this thick, stewlike soup with cornbread, pickle relish and diced sweet onion.

1 pound pinto, yellow-eyed *or* other dried beans, sorted and rinsed (2½ cups)

12 cups water

8 ounces finely diced ham (about 1½ cups)

1 medium onion, peeled

1 clove garlic, peeled

½ teaspoon salt

1 teaspoon ground pepper

¼ teaspoon crushed red pepper

1. Place beans, water, ham, onion, garlic, salt, pepper and crushed red pepper in a large pot; bring to a boil. Reduce heat and simmer, stirring occasionally, until the beans are very tender and beginning to burst, 1½ to 2 hours. If necessary, add an additional ½ to 1 cup water while simmering to keep the beans just submerged in cooking liquid.

2. Remove from the heat; discard the onion and garlic. Transfer 2 cups of the beans to a medium bowl and coarsely mash with a fork or potato masher. Return the mashed beans to the pot; stir to combine.

▸▸ **MAKE AHEAD:** Refrigerate for up to 3 days or freeze for up to 3 months.

SERVES 8: ¾ CUP EACH

Calories 246 | Fat 2g (sat 1g) | Cholesterol 13mg | Carbs 35g | Total sugars 0g (added 0g) | Protein 18g | Fiber 12g | Sodium 517mg | Potassium 682mg.
Nutrition bonus: Folate (58% daily value).

FOUR-BEAN *AND* PUMPKIN CHILI

The bean selection at many markets is bursting with different varieties, and this chili creates the opportunity to buy a few that you've been wanting to try. Pumpkin is a natural addition, because it brings a touch of sweetness along with its otherwise mild flavor.

1 tablespoon extra-virgin olive oil

3 cups chopped onions

1½ cups chopped carrot

3 large cloves garlic, minced

4 cups low-sodium vegetable broth

3 cups diced peeled pumpkin *or* butternut squash

1 28-ounce can no-salt-added crushed tomatoes

4 15-ounce cans low-sodium beans, such as black, great northern, pinto *and/or* red, rinsed

3 tablespoons chili powder

2 teaspoons ground cumin

1 teaspoon ground cinnamon

¾ teaspoon salt

¼ teaspoon cayenne pepper, or to taste

   Cotija cheese (*see Tip*), sliced jalapeños, diced onion *and/or* pepitas for garnish

1. Heat oil in a large pot over medium-high heat. Add onions and cook, stirring often, until starting to brown, about 5 minutes. Reduce heat to medium, add carrot and continue cooking, stirring often, until the vegetables are soft, 4 to 5 minutes more. Add garlic and cook, stirring, for 1 minute.

2. Stir in broth, scraping up any browned bits, and bring to a boil over high heat. Add pumpkin (or squash), tomatoes, beans, chili powder, cumin, cinnamon, salt and cayenne to taste. Cover and return to a boil. Reduce heat to maintain a gentle simmer and cook, uncovered, until the pumpkin (or squash) is tender, about 30 minutes.

3. Serve garnished with cheese, jalapeños, onion and/or pepitas, if desired.

➤ **MAKE AHEAD:** Refrigerate for up to 5 days or freeze for up to 6 months.

SERVES 8: ABOUT 1½ CUPS EACH

Calories 276 | Fat 3g (sat 0g) | Cholesterol 0mg | Carbs 49g | Total sugars 10g (added 0g) | Protein 14g | Fiber 17g | Sodium 509mg | Potassium 1,073mg.
Nutrition bonus: Vitamin A (227% daily value) | Vitamin C (39% dv) | Iron (32% dv) | Folate (20% dv).

Cotija is a crumbly, slightly tangy and pleasantly salty Mexican cheese. If you can't find it, feta makes a perfectly acceptable substitute.

WINTER VEGETABLE DAL

This Southern Indian–inspired dal is rich and creamy thanks to light coconut milk and it gets exotic flavor from coconut oil that you infuse with spices before adding in all the other ingredients. Serve with flatbread or naan. Look for red lentils in the natural-foods section of your supermarket or in natural-foods stores. Garam masala is a blend of cardamom, black pepper, cloves, nutmeg, fennel, cumin and coriander; it is available in the spice section of most supermarkets.

- 2 tablespoons coconut oil *or* canola oil
- 1 teaspoon brown mustard seeds
- 1 teaspoon cumin seeds
- 12 fresh curry leaves (*see Tip*) *or* 1 large bay leaf
- 1 medium onion, finely chopped
- 1 serrano chile, finely diced
- 3 tablespoons finely chopped fresh ginger
- 4 medium cloves garlic, finely chopped
- 4½ cups water
- 1½ cups red lentils, rinsed
- 1 14-ounce can "lite" coconut milk
- 1½ teaspoons salt
- 1 teaspoon ground turmeric
- 2½ cups cubed peeled butternut squash
- 2 cups cauliflower florets (1-inch)
- 1 large Yukon Gold potato (about 8 ounces), cut into ½-inch chunks
- 1 teaspoon garam masala
- 2 tablespoons lime juice

1. Heat oil over medium-high heat in a large pot. Add mustard seeds, cumin seeds and curry leaves (if using) and cook until the seeds begin to pop, about 20 seconds. Add onion, chile, ginger and garlic and cook, stirring occasionally, until the onion is starting to brown, about 5 minutes.

2. Add bay leaf (if using), water, lentils, coconut milk, salt and turmeric to the pot. Bring to a boil, stirring frequently to make sure the lentils don't stick to the bottom. Add squash, cauliflower and potato; return to a boil. Reduce heat to a simmer and cook, uncovered, stirring occasionally, until the vegetables are just tender when pierced with a fork, 20 to 25 minutes.

3. Remove from heat; stir in garam masala and lime juice.

SERVES 6: 1⅔ CUPS EACH

Calories 342 | Fat 10g (sat 7g) | Cholesterol 0mg | Carbs 50g | Total sugars 3g (added 0g) | Protein 15g | Fiber 9g | Sodium 618mg | Potassium 737mg.
Nutrition bonus: Vitamin A (112% daily value) | Vitamin C (48% dv) | Folate (33% dv) | Iron (27% dv).

Find fresh curry leaves in the produce section (and sometimes in the freezer) at Asian markets. Any unused leaves can be frozen, airtight, for up to 2 months.

PORTUGUESE KALE AND RED BEAN SOUP

In its most basic form, this Portuguese soup *(Caldo Verde)* is made with only kale, water, potatoes and linguiça sausage. This version includes kidney beans, tomatoes and carrots to make it more substantial.

1 tablespoon extra-virgin olive oil

10 ounces linguiça *or* andouille sausage *(see Tip)*, halved lengthwise and sliced ¼ inch thick

1 cup chopped onion

1 cup chopped carrot

2 tablespoons finely chopped garlic

6 cups low-sodium chicken broth

1 14-ounce can diced tomatoes

1 tablespoon chopped fresh marjoram *or* thyme

1 pound small white boiling potatoes, halved and sliced ¼ inch thick

1 pound kale *or* other dark leafy greens, stems removed, cut into ¼-inch strips

1 15-ounce can kidney beans, rinsed

½ cup chopped fresh parsley

¼ teaspoon salt

Ground pepper to taste

1. Heat oil in a large pot over medium heat. Add sausage and cook, stirring often, until lightly browned, 4 to 5 minutes. Transfer the sausage to a plate. Add onion and carrot to the pot; cover and cook, stirring occasionally, until soft, 5 to 10 minutes. Stir in garlic and cook 1 minute more. Add broth, tomatoes with their juice and marjoram (or thyme). Cover and bring to a boil. Add potatoes, reduce heat and simmer, uncovered, for 10 minutes.

2. Stir in the reserved sausage, kale (or other greens), beans and parsley. Return to a simmer and cook, stirring often, until the potatoes are tender, 4 to 5 minutes more. Season with salt and pepper.

▸▸ **MAKE AHEAD:** Refrigerate for up to 3 days.

SERVES 8: ABOUT 1⅔ CUPS EACH

Calories 255 | Fat 7g (sat 2g) | Cholesterol 35mg | Carbs 30g | Total sugars 4g (added 0g) | Protein 18g | Fiber 8g | Sodium 442mg | Potassium 930mg.
Nutrition bonus: Vitamin A (146% daily value) | Vitamin C (122% dv) | Folate (24% dv).

Linguiça [*lihng-GWEE-suh*] is a garlicky smoked sausage flavored with paprika that's commonly used in Portuguese and Brazilian cooking. If you can't find it, andouille sausage or smoked Spanish chorizo (not Mexican) makes a delicious substitute.

LOW-CALORIE • VEGETARIAN • GLUTEN-FREE

SOPA TARASCA

This famous soup from the state of Michoacán in Western Mexico is often made with a base of pureed beans along with tomatoes and dried chiles, which bring a lot of the character to the dish. Here we use ancho chiles, which are sweet, earthy and relatively mild. You could also use pasillas, which have a heat level similar to anchos—or, if you like it hot, gaujillos, which also bring some smoky notes to the pot.

1 pound dried pinto beans, soaked overnight

2 tablespoons canola oil

1½ cups diced onions

4 cloves garlic, minced

2 teaspoons ground cumin

1 teaspoon chili powder

6 cups water

3 dried ancho chiles (*see Tip*), stemmed and seeded

1 28-ounce can whole tomatoes

1 teaspoon salt

¼ teaspoon ground pepper

1 ripe avocado, sliced

Crumbled queso fresco, lime wedges & tortilla chips for garnish

1. Drain and rinse beans.

2. Heat oil in a large pot over medium-high heat. Add onions and cook, stirring occasionally, until tender, 3 to 5 minutes. Add garlic, cumin and chili powder; cook, stirring, for 30 seconds. Add the drained beans and water. Bring to a boil over high heat. Reduce heat to maintain a simmer, cover and cook until the beans are tender, 1 to 1½ hours.

3. Meanwhile, soak chiles in boiling water until the skins have softened, about 15 minutes. Drain and chop.

4. Add the chiles, tomatoes and their juice, salt and pepper to the beans. Puree the soup in a regular blender (in batches, if necessary) until very smooth. (Use caution when blending hot liquids.) Serve topped with avocado and garnished with queso fresco, lime wedges and tortilla chips, if desired.

SERVES 8: 1½ CUPS EACH

Calories 319 | Fat 9g (sat 1g) | Cholesterol 0mg | Carbs 48g | Total sugars 5g (added 0g) | Protein 15g | Fiber 14g | Sodium 433mg | Potassium 1,314mg.
Nutrition bonus: Folate (84% daily value) | Vitamin A (37 % dv) | Vitamin C (36 % dv) | Iron (25% dv).

Ancho chiles are dried poblanos— the glossy, dark green chiles traditionally used in chiles rellenos. Anchos have a fruity, moderately spicy and slightly smoky flavor.

FRAGRANT FISH SOUP
P.154

SLIM-DOWN SOUPS

Looking to shed or manage weight? While there's no silver bullet, soups can help. With a high water content, they fill you up and keep you satisfied on fewer calories. In fact, studies show that people tend to consume the fewest calories on days they eat soup. So simmer up a batch of one of these low-calorie soups and give your efforts to slim down a delicious boost!

QUINOA PEANUT SOUP (SOPA DE MANI)

This spicy vegetable, quinoa and peanut soup recipe is a modern take on a traditional Bolivian soup recipe called *sopa de mani*. Make it a heartier meal by adding diced cooked chicken or turkey breast to the soup.

1 tablespoon canola oil

¾ cup chopped onion

2 cloves garlic, minced

1 cup sliced carrots

1 cup diced potatoes

½ cup quinoa

4 cups vegetable broth *or* reduced-sodium chicken broth

2 cups water

½ cup chopped red bell pepper

¼ cup natural peanut butter

1 tablespoon chopped fresh parsley

1 tablespoon hot sauce, such as Tabasco

Ground pepper to taste

1. Heat oil in a large saucepan over medium heat. Add onion and cook, stirring, until softened, 4 to 5 minutes. Stir in garlic and cook, stirring, for 30 seconds. Stir in carrots, potatoes and quinoa, then add broth and water. Bring to a boil over high heat.

2. Reduce heat to maintain a simmer, cover and cook until the quinoa and vegetables are tender, about 18 minutes. Stir in bell pepper and cook, stirring, for 3 minutes more. Stir in peanut butter until it is combined into the broth. Remove from heat. Stir in parsley, hot sauce and pepper.

SERVES 6: ABOUT 1⅓ CUPS EACH

Calories 190 | Fat 9g (sat 1g) | Cholesterol 0mg | Carbs 21g | Total sugars 4g (added 0g) | Protein 6g | Fiber 4g | Sodium 510mg | Potassium 345mg.
Nutrition bonus: Vitamin A (88% daily value) | Vitamin C (38% dv).

TOFU AND VEGETABLE SOUP

Miso and seaweed are both umami ingredients that give this stew a wonderful meaty richness. (Dulse and arame, two of the most common seaweeds used in Asian cooking, can be found in Asian or natural-foods markets.) The addition of eggs, tofu, sweet corn kernels and cabbage results in a well-rounded meal. Use firm silken tofu if you prefer a soft texture; opt for regular firm tofu for more chewiness.

1½ tablespoons canola oil

1 medium onion, chopped

1½ tablespoons grated *or* minced fresh ginger

4 cups thinly sliced napa cabbage

4 cups low-sodium vegetable broth

½ cup snipped dulse *or* arame seaweed

1 cup corn, fresh *or* frozen

2 12- to 14-ounce packages firm tofu, silken *or* regular, drained if necessary, cut into ¼-inch cubes

¼ cup white miso (*see Tip*)

2 large eggs, beaten

4 scallions, chopped

2 tablespoons rice vinegar

1. Heat oil in a large pot over medium-high heat. Add onion and ginger; cook, stirring often, until fragrant, about 1 minute. Add cabbage; cook, stirring occasionally, until starting to wilt, 1 to 2 minutes.

2. Add broth and seaweed; bring to a boil. Reduce heat to medium and simmer for 5 minutes. Add corn, return to a simmer and cook for 2 minutes. Add tofu and cook until hot, about 3 minutes. Stir in miso and cook for 1 minute more.

3. Drizzle eggs onto the surface of the stew and simmer, undisturbed, until just set, 1 to 2 minutes. Remove from heat. Add scallions and vinegar and gently stir to combine.

SERVES 5: ABOUT 2 CUPS EACH

Calories 236 | Fat 10g (sat 2g) | Cholesterol 74mg | Carbs 20g | Total sugars 7g (added 0g) | Protein 14g | Fiber 3g | Sodium 650mg | Potassium 577mg. Nutrition bonus: Vitamin C (26% daily value).

Miso is fermented soybean paste. It's undeniably salty, so a little goes a long way. White or sweet miso (shiromiso), made with soy and rice, is yellow and milder in flavor than red miso. Look for it near tofu at well-stocked supermarkets. It will keep in the refrigerator for at least a year.

OLD-FASHIONED WINTER VEGETABLE CHOWDER

A rice-based sauce cuts the cream out of this creamy chowder. It's already full of vegetables, but you could add sautéed mushrooms or fennel, chopped tomatoes or cubes of roasted squash.

1 teaspoon extra-virgin olive oil plus 1 tablespoon, divided

¼ cup finely chopped onion plus 2 chopped medium onions, divided

3 tablespoons long- *or* medium-grain white rice

5¼ cups reduced-sodium chicken broth, divided, plus more as needed

¼ cup dry white wine

Pinch of salt plus ½ teaspoon, divided

Ground white pepper to taste

⅔ cup diced bacon *or* pancetta

½ cup diced carrot

½ cup diced celery

1 tablespoon chopped garlic

½ teaspoon fennel seed, crushed

1 teaspoon dry mustard

2 cups diced peeled Yukon Gold potatoes

2 cups diced peeled rutabaga

1 cup shredded Monterey Jack, Cheddar *or* Parmesan cheese

3 tablespoons chopped fresh chives *or* scallion greens

1. Heat 1 teaspoon oil in a small saucepan over medium heat. Add finely chopped onion and cook, stirring, until soft but not browned, 3 to 5 minutes. Add rice and cook, stirring, for 1 minute more. Add 1¼ cups broth and wine and bring to a boil. Cover and simmer until the rice is very soft, about 15 minutes.

2. Transfer the mixture to a blender and puree until smooth and pourable; add more broth or water as needed. (Use caution when blending hot liquids.) Season with a pinch of salt and white pepper. Set the sauce aside.

3. Heat a large pot over medium heat and add bacon (or pancetta); cook until browned, 4 to 6 minutes. Transfer to a paper-towel-lined plate; pour off all but 1 tablespoon of the fat.

4. Add the remaining 1 tablespoon oil, chopped onions, carrot, celery, garlic and fennel seed to the pot. Cook, stirring occasionally, until the vegetables are tender and just beginning to color, about 5 minutes. Add dry mustard; cook, stirring, for 1 minute more. Add the remaining 4 cups broth, potatoes and rutabaga. Bring to a boil. Reduce heat to maintain a simmer, cover and cook until the vegetables are just tender, 15 to 20 minutes. Mash a few vegetables against the side and cook for 2 minutes more.

5. Stir in the reserved sauce and heat until steaming. Remove from heat; add cheese and stir until melted. Season with the remaining ½ teaspoon salt and pepper. Serve topped with chives (or scallion greens) and the reserved bacon (or pancetta).

▸▸ **MAKE AHEAD:** Refrigerate sauce (Steps 1-2) and soup (Steps 3-4) separately for up to 3 days or freeze for up to 3 months. Reheat before finishing with Step 5.

SERVES 6: 1⅓ CUPS EACH

Calories 278 | Fat 13g (sat 5g) | Cholesterol 24mg | Carbs 26g | Total sugars 6g (added 0g) | Protein 14g | Fiber 4g | Sodium 532mg | Potassium 727mg. Nutrition bonus: Vitamin A (41% daily value) | Vitamin C (36% dv) | Calcium (20% dv).

Rinse mussels well and use a brush to remove any barnacles. Discard any broken shells. Pull off any fibrous "beard" pinched between the shells.

ORANGE *AND* SAFFRON-SCENTED MUSSEL SOUP

Saffron lends its distinctive floral yet earthy flavor and yellow hue to this elegant soup. It may be the most expensive spice in the world, but there really is nothing else like it—and a little goes a long way. The dried stamens of a type of crocus, saffron has to be harvested by hand—which accounts for its price tag.

1½ tablespoons extra-virgin olive oil

1½ tablespoons butter

3 cloves garlic, minced

4 leeks, white and light green parts only, cleaned and thinly sliced *(see Tip, page 197)*

3 carrots, finely chopped

2 onions, finely chopped

1 bottle (750 ml) dry white wine, such as sauvignon blanc (3 cups)

2 bay leaves

2 teaspoons dried thyme, divided

½ teaspoon ground pepper, plus more to taste

2 cups water

4 pounds fresh mussels, scrubbed and debearded *(see Tip, opposite)*

1 tablespoon orange zest

1 cup orange juice

3 tablespoons flat-leaf parsley, cut into slivers

1 teaspoon saffron threads, crumbled, *or* ¼ teaspoon powdered saffron

½ teaspoon salt

6 plum tomatoes, peeled *(see Tip, page 36)*, seeded and diced

1. Heat oil and butter in a large pot over medium-high heat. Add garlic and cook, stirring, until light golden, about 30 seconds. Add leeks, carrots and onions; cook, stirring occasionally, until very soft, about 15 minutes. Add wine, bay leaves, 1½ teaspoons thyme, ½ teaspoon pepper and water; bring to a simmer. Reduce heat to low and cook for 15 minutes.

2. Stir in mussels, increase heat to medium-high and return to a simmer. Cover the pan and cook for 7 minutes, shaking the pan several times to distribute the mussels. Remove and discard any mussels that do not open.

3. Strain the mussels and cooking liquid through a sieve set over a bowl, pressing hard on the solids to extract all the liquid. Return the liquid to the pot and add orange zest and juice, parsley, saffron and the remaining ½ teaspoon thyme. Season with salt and pepper. Add tomatoes and heat gently (don't boil).

4. To serve, divide the mussels among 8 bowls. (Discard solids remaining in the sieve.) Ladle the broth over the mussels.

SERVES 8: GENEROUS 1 CUP SOUP & 3 OZ. MUSSELS EACH

Calories 319 | Fat 9g (sat 2g) | Cholesterol 48mg | Carbs 25g | Total sugars 9g (added 0g) | Protein 20g | Fiber 3g | Sodium 460mg | Potassium 648mg.
Nutrition bonus: Vitamin B_{12} (302% daily value) | Vitamin A (109% dv) | Iron (39% dv) | Folate (29% dv).

FRAGRANT FISH SOUP

Lemony rice, delicately flavored broth and gently poached tilapia are topped with a colorful blend of vegetables and herbs. The aromatic mint provides fresh and complex flavor. *(Photo: page 144.)*

1 cup jasmine rice

½ teaspoon salt

2 cups water

   Zest and juice of 1 lemon

4 cups low-sodium chicken broth *or* vegetable broth

1 pound tilapia fillets (*see Tip*) *or* other firm white fish, such as cod, red snapper *or* catfish

4 cups bite-size pieces arugula *or* watercress (about 1 bunch), tough stems removed

1 cup finely shredded carrots

¼ cup very thinly sliced fresh mint

2 scallions, finely chopped

1. Combine rice and salt with water in a medium saucepan. Bring to a simmer over medium heat; cover and cook until the water is absorbed, about 20 minutes. Stir in lemon zest and juice.

2. Meanwhile, bring broth to a simmer in another medium saucepan over medium-high heat. Reduce the heat so the broth remains steaming, but not simmering. Add fish and cook until just tender, about 5 minutes. Remove and break into bite-size chunks.

3. Divide the lemony rice among 4 bowls. Top with equal portions of the fish, arugula (or watercress), carrot, mint and scallions. Ladle 1 cup of the warm broth into each bowl and serve.

SERVES 4: ABOUT 1¼ CUPS EACH

Calories 332 | Fat 4g (sat 1g) | Cholesterol 57mg | Carbs 44g | Total sugars 3g (added 0g) | Protein 32g | Fiber 3g | Sodium 453mg | Potassium 776mg.
Nutrition bonus: Vitamin A (106% daily value) | Vitamin B$_{12}$ (34% dv) | Vitamin C (23% dv).

U.S.-farmed tilapia is considered the best choice—it's raised in closed-farming systems that protect nearby ecosystems. Central and South American tilapia is a good alternative.

CRAB BISQUE WITH AVOCADO, TOMATO *AND* CORN RELISH

Our light version of classic crab bisque gets its creaminess from a combination of low-fat milk plus pureed vegetables and potatoes. The tangy, chunky relish provides a texture and flavor contrast to the smoky, rich-tasting bisque. Crabmeat comes canned, in shelf-stable pouches, frozen or pasteurized. Pasteurized has the best flavor; look for it in the fresh seafood section of the market.

RELISH

- 1 small avocado, finely diced
- 1 cup corn, fresh *or* frozen (thawed)
- 1 medium tomato, seeded and finely diced
- 1 tablespoon lime juice
- ¼ teaspoon salt
- Ground pepper to taste

BISQUE

- 1 tablespoon extra-virgin olive oil
- 1 cup corn, fresh *or* frozen (thawed)
- 1 cup chopped onion
- 1 cup diced yellow bell pepper
- 1½ cups diced peeled russet potato
- ¾ teaspoon sweet *or* hot smoked paprika, plus more for garnish
- 1 cup dry sherry
- 2 cups seafood stock *or* broth *or* reduced-sodium chicken broth
- 2 cups low-fat milk
- 12 ounces crabmeat, drained if necessary
- ¼ teaspoon salt

1. To prepare relish: Combine avocado, corn, tomato, lime juice, ¼ teaspoon salt and pepper in a small bowl; toss to coat. Let stand at room temperature while you prepare the bisque.

2. To prepare bisque: Heat oil in a large saucepan over medium heat. Add corn, onion and bell pepper and cook, stirring often, until the onion and pepper have softened, about 5 minutes. Add potato and paprika and cook, stirring often, for 2 minutes. Add sherry and cook, scraping up any browned bits, until the liquid has reduced slightly, about 5 minutes. Add stock (or broth) and bring to a boil. Reduce heat and simmer, stirring occasionally, until the potatoes are very tender, about 15 minutes.

3. Working in two batches, puree the vegetable mixture in a blender or food processor. (Use caution when blending hot liquids.) Return the puree to the saucepan; stir in milk, crab and salt. Cook, stirring occasionally, until heated through, 3 to 5 minutes. Serve topped with the relish and more paprika, if desired.

SERVES 8: ABOUT 1 CUP SOUP & ¼ CUP RELISH EACH

Calories 219 | Fat 7g (sat 1g) | Cholesterol 35mg | Carbs 21g | Total sugars 8g (added 0g) | Protein 15g | Fiber 4g | Sodium 469mg | Potassium 750mg.
Nutrition bonus: Vitamin C (79% daily value) | Vitamin B_{12} (78% dv).

CHICKEN CURRY SOUP

Here's an exotic soup you can make with ingredients you probably have in your pantry. Curry powder, fresh ginger and garlic infuse the soup with all the flavor you need.

1 tablespoon canola oil

1 large onion, chopped

4-5 cloves garlic, crushed

3 slices fresh ginger, peeled and lightly crushed

3 tablespoons curry powder, preferably Madras (*see Tip*)

½ cup white rice

2 bone-in chicken breasts (about 1 pound), skinned and trimmed

4 cups reduced-sodium chicken broth

3 cups water, plus more as needed

1 vine-ripened tomato, seeded and chopped

1 tablespoon lemon juice

Pinch of salt

Pinch of ground pepper

Chopped fresh cilantro *or* chives for garnish

1. Heat oil in a large pot over low heat. Add onion, garlic to taste and ginger; cook, stirring occasionally to prevent browning, until the onion is soft and translucent, 5 to 7 minutes. Add curry powder and rice; cook for 5 minutes more.

2. Add chicken, broth and 3 cups water. Bring to a boil, then reduce heat to medium. Simmer, stirring frequently, until the chicken is no longer pink in the center, about 30 minutes. Transfer the chicken to a plate to cool.

3. Puree the soup in batches in a food processor until smooth, adding water as needed for a creamy texture. (Use caution when blending hot liquids.) Return the soup to the pot and bring to a simmer over medium heat.

4. Shred the chicken and add to the soup along with tomato; cook for 3 minutes more. Season with lemon juice, salt and pepper. Serve topped with cilantro (or chives), if desired.

SERVES 6: 1⅓ CUPS EACH

Calories 189 | Fat 4g (sat 1g) | Cholesterol 34mg | Carbs 21g | Total sugars 2g (added 0g) | Protein 17g | Fiber 2g | Sodium 431mg | Potassium 389mg.

Madras curry powder is earthy, fragrant and just a little bit hotter than the stuff simply labeled "curry powder" in the spice aisle. It originated in Southern India, in the city called Madras (same as the famed fabric) under British rule, now called Chennai.

ITALIAN EGG-DROP SOUP

Stracciatella is a light Italian soup traditionally made with just chicken broth, eggs and herbs. For our version, we add whole-grain pasta, chickpeas and arugula to make it heartier.

6 cups low-sodium chicken broth

2 cups water

1⅓ cups whole-wheat medium pasta shells *or* other small pasta (4 ounces)

⅔ cup canned chickpeas, rinsed

1 bunch scallions, sliced, whites and greens divided

Pinch of freshly grated nutmeg

3 cups chopped arugula, any tough stems removed

4 large eggs, lightly beaten

Ground pepper to taste

2 tablespoons lemon juice

6 tablespoons freshly grated Parmesan cheese

1. Combine broth, water, pasta, chickpeas, scallion whites and nutmeg in a large pot; cover and bring to a boil over high heat. Uncover and boil for half as long as directed by the pasta package, 3 to 5 minutes.

2. Stir in arugula and cook until wilted, about 1 minute. Reduce heat to low. While stirring the soup constantly, slowly add eggs; cook for 2 minutes. (The cooked egg will look like feathery strands.) Season with pepper and stir in the scallion greens and lemon juice. Serve topped with Parmesan.

SERVES 6: ABOUT 1½ CUPS EACH

Calories 221 | Fat 7g (sat 2g) | Cholesterol 128mg | Carbs 27g | Total sugars 2g (added 0g) | Protein 16g | Fiber 3g | Sodium 235mg | Potassium 437mg.

CELERY AND PARMESAN MINESTRONE

This simple soup cooks quickly with celery stalks, leaves and dried celery seeds to flavor the delicious Parmesan-laced tomato broth.

 2   **tablespoons extra-virgin olive oil**
 2   **cups diced celery**
 ½   **cup diced carrot**
 ½   **cup diced onion**
 1   **clove garlic, chopped**
 1   **teaspoon celery seeds**
 ½   **teaspoon ground pepper**
 4   **cups reduced-sodium chicken broth
      or vegetable broth**
 ⅓   **cup whole-wheat orzo _or_ other small pasta**
 1   **15-ounce can diced tomatoes**
1¾   **cups cooked chickpeas _or_ cannellini beans
      _or_ one 15-ounce can, rinsed**
 ½   **cup chopped celery leaves, divided (_see Tip_)**
 ¼   **cup packed grated Parmigiano-Reggiano
      cheese, plus more for serving**

1. Heat oil in a large saucepan or pot over medium heat. Add celery, carrot, onion, garlic, celery seeds and pepper. Cook, stirring occasionally, until the vegetables are tender, about 10 minutes.

2. Add broth and bring to a boil. Add pasta and cook, uncovered, until the pasta is tender, 8 to 10 minutes. Add tomatoes, chickpeas (or beans), half the celery leaves and ¼ cup Parmigiano-Reggiano. Cook over medium heat until steaming hot, 3 to 5 minutes. Ladle into bowls and garnish with the remaining celery leaves and more cheese, if desired.

➤➤ **MAKE AHEAD:** Refrigerate for up to 1 day.

SERVES 6: ABOUT 1¼ CUPS EACH

Calories 198 | Fat 7g (sat 1g) | Cholesterol 3mg | Carbs 24g | Total sugars 3g (added 0g) | Protein 10g | Fiber 6g | Sodium 580mg | Potassium 570mg.
Nutrition bonus: Vitamin A (47% daily value) | Folate (21% dv).

Celery leaves are an under-appreciated ingredient. They have a fresh, intense celery flavor and can be treated like any fresh herb—even as the star ingredient in a celery-leaf pesto.

SOUTHWESTERN VEGETABLE *AND* CHICKEN SOUP

This delicious soup is absolutely loaded with vegetables—peppers, green beans, chard, corn and tomatoes. If you feel like it, by all means try it with other vegetables instead.

2 medium poblano peppers

1 tablespoon canola oil

12 ounces boneless, skinless chicken thighs, trimmed, cut into bite-size pieces

1½ cups chopped onion

1½ cups chopped red *or* green bell pepper

1½ cups green beans, cut into ¼-inch pieces, fresh *or* frozen, thawed

4 cloves garlic, minced

1 tablespoon chili powder

1½ teaspoons ground cumin

6 cups low-sodium chicken broth

1 15-ounce can black beans *or* pinto beans, rinsed

1 14-ounce can diced tomatoes

4 cups chopped chard *or* spinach

1½ cups corn, fresh *or* frozen (thawed)

½ teaspoon salt

½ cup fresh lime juice, plus lime wedges for garnish

½ cup chopped fresh cilantro

1. Position oven rack about 5 inches from the heat source; preheat broiler. Line the broiler pan with foil. Broil poblanos, turning once, until starting to blacken, 8 to 12 minutes. Transfer to a paper bag and let steam to loosen skins, about 10 minutes. When the poblanos are cool enough to handle, peel, seed, stem and coarsely chop; set aside.

2. Meanwhile, heat oil in a large pot over medium-high heat. Add chicken and cook, stirring occasionally, until lightly browned, 3 to 5 minutes. Transfer to a plate and set aside.

3. Reduce heat to medium and add onion, bell pepper, green beans and garlic. Cook, stirring, until beginning to soften, 5 to 7 minutes. Stir in chili powder and cumin and cook, stirring, until fragrant, about 30 seconds. Stir in broth, beans, tomatoes and the chopped poblanos; bring to a boil. Reduce heat to maintain a simmer and cook, stirring occasionally, until the vegetables are tender, about 15 minutes.

4. Add the reserved chicken and any accumulated juices, chard (or spinach), corn and salt; return to a simmer and cook for 15 minutes more to blend flavors.

5. Stir in lime juice. Top with cilantro and serve with lime wedges, if desired.

➤ **MAKE AHEAD:** Prepare through Step 4 and refrigerate for up to 3 days or freeze for up to 6 months; add lime juice and cilantro just before serving.

SERVES 8: ABOUT 1½ CUPS EACH

Calories 213 | Fat 6g (sat 1g) | Cholesterol 39mg | Carbs 25g | Total sugars 7g (added 0g) | Protein 17g | Fiber 6g | Sodium 386mg | Potassium 779mg.
Nutrition bonus: Vitamin C (121% daily value) | Vitamin A (56% dv).

BORSCHT WITH BEEF

Even people who think they don't like beets love this vibrant vegetable-packed soup. The legendary dish served at New York City's Russian Tea Room was the inspiration for this version.

- 4 teaspoons canola oil, divided
- 8 ounces sirloin *or* flank steak, trimmed, cut into ½-inch cubes
- 8 ounces mushrooms, sliced
- 4 medium beets (about 1 pound), peeled and shredded (*see Tip*)
- 1½ cups shredded cabbage
- 1 cup shredded carrots
- 1 cup finely chopped onion
- 1 cup finely chopped celery
- ½ cup dry red wine
- 6 cups reduced-sodium beef broth
- 1 cup no-salt-added tomato sauce
- 1 tablespoon Worcestershire sauce
- ¼ cup chopped fresh dill, plus more for garnish
- ½ cup reduced-fat sour cream

1. Heat 2 teaspoons oil in a large pot over medium-high heat. Add steak and cook, stirring frequently, until beginning to brown, 2 to 4 minutes. Transfer to a bowl.

2. Add 1 teaspoon oil to the pot and heat over medium-high. Add mushrooms and cook, stirring, until beginning to brown, 3 to 5 minutes. Transfer to the bowl.

3. Add the remaining 1 teaspoon oil to the pot. Add beets, cabbage, carrots, onion and celery. Cook, stirring frequently, until beginning to soften, about 10 minutes. Add wine and cook, stirring and scraping up any browned bits. Stir in the reserved mushrooms, broth, tomato sauce and Worcestershire. Cover and bring to a boil. Reduce heat to maintain a simmer and cook, covered, until the vegetables are very tender, about 30 minutes.

4. Add the reserved beef. Simmer, covered, until heated through, 1 to 2 minutes. Stir in ¼ cup dill. Top each portion with 1 tablespoon sour cream and garnish with more dill, if desired.

▸▸ **MAKE AHEAD:** Refrigerate for up to 3 days; garnish just before serving.

SERVES 8: ABOUT 1⅓ CUPS EACH

Calories 149 | Fat 6g (sat 2g) | Cholesterol 24mg | Carbs 13g | Total sugars 7g (added 0g) | Protein 10g | Fiber 3g | Sodium 434mg | Potassium 657mg.
Nutrition bonus: Vitamin A (52% daily value) | Vitamin C (21% dv).

PLUGGED-IN SOUPS

If there is one type of food that's perfectly suited to a slow cooker, it's soup. The longer it simmers, the better it tastes—and there are no watched pots. You can walk away and come home to a house that smells superb and a dinner that's ready and waiting.

CHICKEN-CORN
TORTILLA SOUP
P.168

LOW-CALORIE • GLUTEN-FREE

CHICKEN-CORN TORTILLA SOUP

Using bone-in chicken thighs in this soup ensures the meat stays moist over the long cooking time. Not only are chicken thighs inherently juicier than breast meat, but cooking chicken on the bone also helps it stay succulent. *(Photo: page 167.)*

EQUIPMENT: 5- TO 6-QUART SLOW COOKER

- 2 **cups chopped onion**
- 2 **Anaheim *or* jalapeño peppers (*see Tip*), seeded and chopped**
- 1 **red bell pepper, seeded and chopped**
- 2 **cloves garlic, minced**
- 2 **pounds bone-in chicken thighs, skin removed**
- 4 **cups low-sodium chicken broth**
- 3 **cups water**
- 1 **15-ounce can fire-roasted diced tomatoes**
- 1½ **teaspoons ground cumin**
- 1½ **teaspoons crushed dried oregano**
- ½ **teaspoon ground coriander**
- ½ **teaspoon salt**
- 2 **bay leaves**
- 1 **cup lightly crushed tortilla chips, plus more for serving**
- ½ **cup corn, fresh *or* frozen (thawed)**
- 2 **teaspoons lime zest**
- 2 **tablespoons lime juice**
  Diced avocado, shredded Cheddar cheese, sour cream *and/or* lime wedges for garnish

1. Combine onion, Anaheim (or jalapeño) pepper, bell pepper and garlic in a 5- to 6-quart slow cooker. Arrange chicken over the vegetables. Add broth, water, tomatoes, cumin, oregano, coriander, salt and bay leaves. Cover and cook on High for 3½ hours or on Low for 8 hours.

2. Carefully transfer the chicken to a clean cutting board. Shred with 2 forks (discard the bones).

3. Meanwhile, stir tortilla chips and corn into the slow cooker. If using the Low setting, turn to High. Cover and cook for 30 minutes more.

4. Stir the soup, breaking up any remaining pieces of tortilla chips. Stir in the chicken, lime zest and lime juice. Serve the soup with more tortilla chips, avocado, cheese, sour cream and/or lime wedges, if desired.

➤➤ **PREP AHEAD:** Chop onion, peppers and garlic and combine. Combine broth, water, tomatoes and spices. Refrigerate in separate containers for up to 1 day.

SERVES 8: 1½ CUPS EACH

Calories 207 | Fat 8g (sat 2g) | Cholesterol 57mg | Carbs 14g | Total sugars 5g (added 0g) | Protein 20g | Fiber 3g | Sodium 369mg | Potassium 469mg.
Nutrition bonus: Vitamin C (47% daily value).

Anaheim chiles are bright, fresh and peppery. They bring a little bit of heat to the table, but not too much. If you want more fire, use jalapeños instead.

BASQUE CHICKEN STEW

Straddling the coastal border between Northern Spain and Southern France, the people of the Basque region have a deep affection for fork-tender chicken stewed in a vibrant tomato-pepper sauce. Briny green olives stuffed with Spain's pimiento peppers root the dish even further.

EQUIPMENT: 5- TO 6-QUART SLOW COOKER

- 2 **pounds skinless, boneless chicken thighs, trimmed and cut into 2-inch pieces**
- 1½ **pounds red potatoes, cut into ½-inch-wide wedges**
- 1 **large onion, thinly sliced**
- 1 **large red bell pepper, sliced**
- 1 **28-ounce can diced tomatoes, drained**
- 1 **cup low-sodium chicken broth**
- 4 **cloves garlic, minced**
- 2 **teaspoons chopped fresh thyme**
- 1 **teaspoon salt**
- ½ **teaspoon ground pepper**
- ½ **teaspoon crushed dried savory**
- ½ **cup small pimiento-stuffed olives**

1. Combine chicken, potatoes, onion and bell pepper in a 5- to 6-quart slow cooker. Stir in tomatoes, broth, garlic, thyme, salt, pepper and savory. Cover and cook on High for 4 hours or on Low for 8 hours.

2. Stir in olives before serving.

➤ **PREP AHEAD:** Prep chicken, onion and bell pepper and combine. Prep potatoes and cover with water. Combine tomatoes, broth, garlic, thyme, salt, pepper and savory. Refrigerate separately for up to 1 day.

SERVES 8: 1½ CUPS EACH

Calories 246 | Fat 8g (sat 2g) | Cholesterol 104mg | Carbs 20g | Total sugars 4g (added 0g) | Protein 23g | Fiber 3g | Sodium 685mg | Potassium 860mg. Nutrition bonus: Vitamin C (77% daily value) | Vitamin A (23% dv).

LOW-CALORIE • GLUTEN-FREE

MULLIGATAWNY SOUP

This is a soup with a long history (references to it in English go back to 1784) that can now be conveniently made in a modern appliance. Although it's technically an English soup, its origins are decidedly Indian. (The name loosely means "pepper water" in the Tamil language of Southern India.) The sweetness of apple and coconut milk counterbalances the garlic, ginger, curry and cayenne.

EQUIPMENT: 5- TO 6-QUART SLOW COOKER

- 2 pounds boneless, skinless chicken thighs, trimmed
- 1 large yellow onion, coarsely chopped
- 4 carrots, chopped
- 4 stalks celery, chopped
- 2 green apples, chopped, plus more for serving
- 2 tablespoons grated fresh ginger
- 4 cloves garlic, sliced
- 2 tablespoons curry powder
- ½ teaspoon salt
- ¼ teaspoon cayenne pepper
- 4 cups low-sodium chicken broth
- 1 cup brown basmati *or* jasmine rice (*see Tip, opposite*)
- 1 14-ounce can "lite" coconut milk
- ¼ cup chopped fresh cilantro, plus more for serving

1. Combine chicken, onion, carrots, celery, apples, ginger, garlic, curry powder, salt and cayenne in a 5- to 6-quart slow cooker. Add broth. Cover and cook on High for 2 hours or Low for 4 hours.

2. If using the Low setting, turn to High. Add rice. Cover and cook for 1 hour more.

3. Remove the chicken to a clean cutting board. Add coconut milk and cilantro to the soup. Shred the chicken into bite-size pieces with 2 forks and return to the soup. Serve topped with more cilantro and diced apple, if desired.

➤ **PREP AHEAD:** Chop onion, carrots and celery and combine with grated ginger, sliced garlic, spices and salt. Refrigerate for up to 1 day.

SERVES 8: 1¾ CUPS EACH

Calories 325 | Fat 12g (sat 5g) | Cholesterol 104mg | Carbs 31g | Total sugars 7g (added 0g) | Protein 25g | Fiber 5g | Sodium 316mg | Potassium 574mg.
Nutrition bonus: Vitamin A (106% daily value).

While nutty and aromatic basmati rice— with its Indian origin— might be more traditional in this soup, delicate and floral jasmine rice works too.

SWEDISH YELLOW SPLIT PEA SOUP WITH HAM

Over the cooking time, the split peas break down just the right amount to create a creamy, almost-pureed texture. If you like, do as the Swedes do and top each serving with a spoonful of spicy brown mustard.

EQUIPMENT: 5- TO 6-QUART SLOW COOKER

- 3 cups yellow split peas (about 1½ pounds)
- 4 cups reduced-sodium chicken broth
- 4 cups water
- 2 cups diced yellow onion
- 1 cup diced carrot
- 1 cup finely diced celery
- 8 ounces ham steak, trimmed and diced
- 1 tablespoon minced fresh ginger
- 1 teaspoon dried marjoram
- Ground pepper to taste

1. Place split peas in a medium bowl. Rinse with cold water until the water runs clear; drain and spread in a 5- to 6-quart slow cooker.

2. Add broth, water, onion, carrot, celery, ham, ginger and marjoram to the slow cooker. Stir to combine.

3. Cover and cook for 5 hours on High or 7 to 8 hours on Low. Season with pepper.

➤ **PREP AHEAD:** Prep split peas, onion, carrot, celery and ginger. Dice ham. Refrigerate separately for up to 1 day.

SERVES 8: ABOUT 1½ CUPS EACH

Calories 335 | Fat 2g (sat 1g) | Cholesterol 13mg | Carbs 55g | Total sugars 5g (added 0g) | Protein 24g | Fiber 20g | Sodium 663mg | Potassium 1,098mg.
Nutrition bonus: Vitamin A (55% daily value) | Iron (25% dv) | Vitamin C (23% dv).

LENTIL AND ROOT VEGGIE SOUP

French green lentils and black lentils hold up well to long, slow cooking without becoming mushy. Save the rinds from used-up blocks of Parmesan in a resealable plastic bag or tightly sealed container in the refrigerator. They give broth for soups a rich, savory flavor.

EQUIPMENT: 5- TO 6-QUART SLOW COOKER

- 3 cups chopped peeled celeriac (celery root)
- 2 cups chopped parsnips
- 1 cup chopped carrot
- 1 cup frozen pearl onions
- 1 stalk celery, chopped
- 2 plum tomatoes, seeded and chopped
- 3 cloves garlic, minced
- 2 teaspoons herbes de Provence
- 8 cups low-sodium chicken broth *or* vegetable broth
- 1 cup French green lentils *or* black lentils, rinsed
- 1 sprig fresh rosemary
- 1 3-inch Parmesan cheese rind plus ½ cup grated Parmesan, divided
- 1 bay leaf
- 1 teaspoon salt
- ½ teaspoon ground pepper
- 4 ounces pancetta, crisp-cooked and crumbled (optional)

1. Combine celeriac, parsnips, carrot, pearl onions, celery, tomatoes, garlic and herbes de Provence in a 5- to 6-quart slow cooker. Add broth, lentils, rosemary, Parmesan rind, bay leaf, salt and pepper. Cover and cook on High for 4½ hours or on Low for 8 hours.

2. Remove the rosemary, Parmesan rind and bay leaf. Serve the soup topped with grated cheese and garnished with pancetta, if desired.

➤ **PREP AHEAD:** Chop celeriac, parsnips, carrot, celery and tomatoes and combine with onions and minced garlic. Refrigerate for up to 1 day.

SERVES 8: 1¾ CUPS EACH

Calories 187 | Fat 3g (sat 1g) | Cholesterol 4mg | Carbs 28g | Total sugars 6g (added 0g) | Protein 13g | Fiber 6g | Sodium 528mg | Potassium 645mg.
Nutrition bonus: Vitamin A (57% daily value) | Vitamin C (25% dv).

MOROCCAN LENTIL SOUP

A long cooking time allows the spices to work their way into the lentils and vegetables, creating a fragrant soup. If you make it ahead, the flavors will have more time to develop.

EQUIPMENT: 5- TO 6-QUART SLOW COOKER

- **2 cups chopped onions**
- **2 cups chopped carrots**
- **4 cloves garlic, minced**
- **2 teaspoons extra-virgin olive oil**
- **1 teaspoon ground cumin**
- **1 teaspoon ground coriander**
- **1 teaspoon ground turmeric**
- **¼ teaspoon ground cinnamon**
- **¼ teaspoon ground pepper**
- **6 cups vegetable broth** *or* **reduced-sodium chicken broth**
- **2 cups water**
- **3 cups chopped cauliflower**
- **1¾ cups French green lentils** *or* **brown lentils**
- **1 28-ounce can diced tomatoes**
- **2 tablespoons tomato paste**
- **4 cups chopped fresh spinach** *or* **10 ounces frozen chopped spinach, thawed**
- **½ cup chopped fresh cilantro**
- **2 tablespoons lemon juice**

1. Combine onions, carrots, garlic, oil, cumin, coriander, turmeric, cinnamon and pepper in a 5- to 6-quart slow cooker. Add broth, water, cauliflower, lentils, tomatoes and tomato paste and stir until well combined.

2. Cover and cook until the lentils are tender, 4 to 5 hours on High or 8 to 10 hours on Low.

3. Add spinach to the slow cooker. Stir, cover and cook on High for 30 minutes.

4. Just before serving, stir in cilantro and lemon juice.

▸▸ **PREP AHEAD:** Prep onions, carrots, garlic and cauliflower. Combine spices. Refrigerate separately for up to 1 day.

▸▸ **MAKE AHEAD:** Prepare through Step 3 and refrigerate for up to 3 days or freeze for up to 6 months. To serve, reheat and stir in cilantro and lemon juice.

SERVES 8: ABOUT 1⅔ CUPS EACH

Calories 228 | Fat 2g (sat 0g) | Cholesterol 0mg | Carbs 41g | Total sugars 10g (added 0g) | Protein 14g | Fiber 14g | Sodium 694mg | Potassium 1,058mg.
Nutrition bonus: Vitamin A (150% daily value) | Folate & Vitamin C (70% dv) | Iron (21% dv).

SPANISH CHICKPEA SOUP

Each region, family and restaurant in Spain has its own variation, but this version of *cocido* has enough meat to satisfy the carnivores and enough vegetables to keep it healthy. Ask for a 4-ounce slab of Serrano ham or prosciutto at your deli counter instead of buying slices.

EQUIPMENT: 6-QUART (OR LARGER) SLOW COOKER

- 1 pound dried chickpeas
- 6 chicken drumsticks (about 2 pounds), skin removed
- 1 4-ounce piece Serrano ham *or* prosciutto, cut into ½-inch cubes
- 4 ounces Spanish-style chorizo, cut into ½-inch rounds
- 8 baby red potatoes, scrubbed and halved
- 1 large leek, white and light green parts, halved and thinly sliced *(see Tip, page 197)*
- 2 medium carrots, cut into ½-inch chunks
- 2 stalks celery, chopped
- 3 large cloves garlic, minced
- 2 bay leaves
- 1 tablespoon chopped fresh oregano
- 1 tablespoon smoked paprika, preferably Pimentón de la Vera
- ½ teaspoon saffron threads *or* ¼ teaspoon powdered saffron
- 6 cups low-sodium chicken broth
- ½ medium cabbage (about 1 pound), cored and cut into 8 wedges
- Ground pepper to taste
- ½ cup chopped fresh parsley

1. Soak chickpeas in enough cold water to cover by 2 inches for at least 12 hours and up to 1 day.

2. Place chicken in a 6-quart (or larger) slow cooker. Drain the chickpeas and add along with ham (or prosciutto), chorizo, potatoes, leek, carrots, celery, garlic, bay leaves, oregano, paprika and saffron. Bring broth to a boil in a saucepan, then pour it into the slow cooker. Cover and cook on High for 4 hours.

3. Transfer the chicken to a clean cutting board. Nestle cabbage into the soup, cover and cook on High until it is tender, about 30 minutes. Discard the bay leaves. Remove the chicken from the bones and stir it back into the soup; season with pepper. Serve sprinkled with parsley.

➤➤ **PREP AHEAD:** Soak chickpeas up to 1 day ahead. Prep chicken. Prep potatoes and cover with water. Prep leek, carrots, celery and garlic. Prep ham and chorizo. Refrigerate separately for up to 1 day.

➤➤ **MAKE AHEAD:** Refrigerate soup for up to 3 days.

SERVES 8: 2 CUPS EACH

Calories 469 | Fat 15g (sat 4g) | Cholesterol 99mg | Carbs 49g | Total sugars 10g (added 0g) | Protein 38g | Fiber 13g | Sodium 733mg | Potassium 1,216mg. Nutrition bonus: Vitamin A (72% daily value) | Vitamin C (58% dv) | Iron (34% dv).

LAMB AND ROOT VEGETABLE STEW WITH GREMOLATA

Gremolata—an herb garnish traditionally made with lemon, parsley and garlic—is the classic finish for osso buco (braised veal shanks). It adds bright flavor to the luxuriously rich dish. This version made with orange instead of lemon does the same for this hearty lamb stew.

EQUIPMENT: 5- TO 6-QUART SLOW COOKER

STEW

- 3 pounds lamb stew meat, trimmed and cut into bite-size pieces
- 6 cups chopped root vegetables (1-inch), such as carrot, parsnip, turnip, rutabaga, Yukon Gold potato *and/or* sweet potato
- 4 cloves garlic, minced
- 4 cups reduced-sodium beef broth
- 1 cup dry red wine
- 6 tablespoons tomato paste
- 4 teaspoons Dijon mustard
- 1 tablespoon chopped fresh rosemary
- 1 tablespoon chopped fresh thyme
- ½ teaspoon salt
- ½ teaspoon ground pepper
- 6 tablespoons cold water
- 2 tablespoons plus 2 teaspoons cornstarch
- 4 cups frozen pearl onions

ORANGE GREMOLATA

- 1 orange, zested
- ⅓ cup chopped fresh parsley
- 1 clove garlic, minced
- ⅛ teaspoon salt
- ⅛ teaspoon ground pepper

1. To prepare stew: Place lamb in a 5- to 6-quart slow cooker. Top with root vegetables and garlic cloves. Combine broth, wine, tomato paste, mustard, rosemary, thyme and ½ teaspoon each salt and pepper in a large bowl. Pour into the slow cooker. Cover and cook on High for 4 hours or Low for 8 hours.

2. If using the Low setting, turn to High. Combine water and cornstarch and stir into the stew. Add pearl onions. Cover and cook until thickened and the onions are tender, about 20 minutes.

3. Meanwhile, prepare gremolata: Combine orange zest, parsley, garlic, salt and pepper. Serve the stew topped with the gremolata.

▸▸ **PREP AHEAD:** Prep lamb. Mince garlic and combine with broth, wine, tomato paste, mustard, herbs, salt and pepper. Refrigerate separately for up to 1 day.

SERVES 12: 1¼ CUPS STEW & 1½ TSP. GREMOLATA EACH

Calories 249 | Fat 6g (sat 4g) | Cholesterol 74mg | Carbs 18g | Total sugars 6g (added 0g) | Protein 25g | Fiber 3g | Sodium 489mg | Potassium 754mg.
Nutrition bonus: Vitamin A (73% daily value) | Vitamin B_{12} (50% dv) | Vitamin C (28% dv).

If you'd like, brown the meat in 1 tablespoon olive oil in two batches in a large skillet before adding to the slow cooker. This intensifies the meat flavor.

FRENCH ONION SOUP

The secret to this intensely flavored soup is that two types of onions are caramelized for hours in the slow cooker before adding a sherry-spiked broth. For a bistro-worthy presentation, ladle the soup into ovenproof crocks, top with the bread and cheese and broil.

EQUIPMENT: 6- TO 7-QUART SLOW COOKER

- 2 **tablespoons butter, cut into 8 pieces**
- 2 **tablespoons extra-virgin olive oil**
- 8 **sprigs fresh thyme**
- 4 **cloves garlic, smashed**
- 1 **bay leaf**
- 2 **pounds yellow onions, halved and sliced** (*see Tip*)
- 2 **pounds red onions, halved and sliced**
- 1 **teaspoon salt**
- ¾ **teaspoon ground pepper**
- 4 **cups low-sodium beef broth**
- ¼ **cup dry sherry**

CHEESE TOASTS

- 8 **diagonal slices baguette (½-inch-thick), toasted**
- 1 **cup shredded Gruyère** *or* **Swiss cheese**

1. To prepare soup: Scatter butter in a 6- to 7-quart slow cooker. Add oil, thyme, garlic and bay leaf, then onions. Sprinkle with salt and pepper. Cover and cook on High for 8 hours.

2. Bring broth and sherry to a boil in a saucepan. Remove the thyme sprigs and bay leaf from the slow cooker. Pour in the broth and cook on High, uncovered, for 10 minutes.

3. To prepare cheese toasts: Meanwhile, position rack in upper third of oven; preheat broiler to high. Top each baguette slice with 2 tablespoons cheese. Broil until the cheese is melted, 1 to 2 minutes. Divide the soup among 8 bowls. Top each with a cheese toast.

➤➤ **PREP AHEAD:** Refrigerate sliced onions for up to 1 day.

➤➤ **MAKE AHEAD:** Refrigerate soup (Steps 1-2) for up to 5 days or freeze for up to 3 months. Make cheese toasts before serving.

SERVES 8: ABOUT 1 CUP SOUP & 1 TOAST EACH

Calories 271 | Fat 12g (sat 5g) | Cholesterol 22mg | Carbs 31g | Total sugars 9g (added 0g) | Protein 12g | Fiber 5g | Sodium 529mg | Potassium 428mg
Nutrition bonus: Vitamin C (26% daily value).

To take the tears out of onion prep, refrigerate whole, unpeeled onions for about 30 minutes before slicing or chopping. The cold "chills out" the sulfur compounds that can irritate your eyes and make you cry.

SHIITAKE *AND* NOODLE HOT *AND* SOUR SOUP

Dried mushrooms rehydrate as you slow-cook this classic Chinese soup, giving the broth deep umami flavor. With the addition of cooked noodles at the end, it's a satisfying vegetarian meal.

EQUIPMENT: 6-QUART (OR LARGER) SLOW COOKER

- 24 dried shiitake *or* black Chinese mushrooms (2-3 ounces)
- 2 carrots, cut into ½-by-2-inch sticks
- 2 8-ounce cans bamboo shoots, rinsed
- 2 14-ounce packages extra-firm water-packed tofu, drained and cut into ½-inch pieces
- 1 teaspoon ground white pepper
- 4 cups thinly sliced green cabbage
- 4⅓ cups water, divided
- 4 cups mushroom *or* vegetable broth
- ¼ cup white vinegar *or* rice vinegar
- ¼ cup red-wine vinegar
- ¼ cup reduced-sodium soy sauce, plus more to taste
- 1 tablespoon chile-garlic sauce, plus more to taste
- 1 tablespoon minced fresh ginger
- 3 tablespoons cornstarch
- 1 tablespoon toasted sesame oil
- 3 cups cooked lo mein noodles (about 6 ounces dry)
- 1 cup sliced scallions

1. Discard mushroom stems and cut the caps into ½-inch pieces. Spread the mushroom pieces in a 6-quart (or larger) slow cooker. Add carrots, bamboo shoots and tofu to slow cooker; sprinkle with white pepper. Top with cabbage.

2. Combine 4 cups water, broth, white (or rice) vinegar, red-wine vinegar, soy sauce, chile-garlic sauce and ginger in a bowl; add to the slow cooker.

3. Cover and cook for 4 hours on High or 7 to 8 hours on Low.

4. Whisk the remaining ⅓ cup water, cornstarch and sesame oil in a bowl. Stir into the soup. If using the Low setting, turn to High. Cover and cook for 20 minutes. Stir in noodles, cover and cook for 10 minutes more. Serve topped with scallions and with more soy sauce and chile-garlic sauce, if desired.

➤➤ **PREP AHEAD:** Prep mushrooms and vegetables; combine the liquids and ginger used in Step 2. Refrigerate separately for up to 1 day.

SERVES 8: ABOUT 2 CUPS EACH

Calories 239 | Fat 7g (sat 1g) | Cholesterol 0mg | Carbs 32g | Total sugars 3g (added 0g) | Protein 14g | Fiber 4g | Sodium 683mg | Potassium 431mg.
Nutrition bonus: Vitamin A (54% daily value) | Calcium (32% dv) | Vitamin C (28% dv).

BREADSTICKS, HACKED

Here's how to put bakery-fresh breadsticks beside your bowl of soup without a lick of mixing or kneading. Start with store-bought whole-wheat pizza dough and combine with one of these 8 flavor-sprinkle options. Homemade soup and bread? It's not as hard as you think.

1 pound pizza dough, preferably whole-wheat

1½ tablespoons extra-virgin olive oil

4 tablespoons topping combination *(see variations)*

1. Arrange racks in upper and lower thirds of oven; preheat to 400°F. Line 2 baking sheets with parchment paper or coat with cooking spray.

2. Divide dough into 16 equal pieces and roll each into a 12- to 14-inch-long breadstick. Place the breadsticks at least ½ inch apart on the baking sheets. Brush with oil and sprinkle with topping, pressing if necessary to help it stick.

3. Bake the breadsticks on the upper and lower racks, switching the pans halfway through, until light brown, 15 to 20 minutes. Transfer to wire racks to cool.

CHIVES
(3 TBSP)
+
GARLIC
POWDER
(1 TBSP)

PECORINO
CHEESE
(3 TBSP)
+
ITALIAN
SEASONING
(1 TBSP)

MANCHEGO
CHEESE
(3 TBSP)
+
CHILI
POWDER
(1 TBSP)

ROSEMARY
+
GARLIC
POWDER
(2 TBSP
EACH)

SESAME
SEEDS
+
FENNEL
SEEDS
(2 TBSP
EACH)

POPPY
SEEDS
+
ONION
POWDER
(2 TBSP
EACH)

PARMESAN
(3 TBSP)
+
BASIL
(1 TBSP)

ASIAGO
CHEESE
(3 TBSP)
+
OREGANO
(1 TBSP)

SOUP SOCIAL

The idea is simple: Ask each guest to make a big batch of soup and bring it to a kind of soup swap meet. Pour some wine, catch up, tell stories and laugh. Everyone goes home with a variety of soups for the fridge or freezer—and the lingering warmth of friendship.

THE SOUP SWAP

By Kathy Gunst

A few years back, a friend called and asked me to be part of a soup swap. I figured it was just another version of a potluck (and, after living in New England for over 30 years, I am just plain old sick of potlucks), but I let her explain. What if we each made a large pot of soup, got together at a different person's home each winter month and had a party? At the end of the night, she said, we all go home with many different types of soup. You cook once, get to hang out with friends, and fill your fridge and freezer with a bunch of meals. Do the math. It's a win-win.

Winter in my small town in southern Maine can be cold, gloomy and isolating. A soup swap sounded like a great way to give the season new focus. All that winter (and for years after), 12 of us got together on the second Sunday of each month. Bundled up, we trekked through blizzards and sub-zero temperatures schlepping pots of soups to one another's kitchens.

At first the soups were basic—chicken noodle, tomato, vegetable purees. But everyone became more adventurous with each swap. "I started using new herbs and spices, and got into experimenting," said a friend in our group. "I just started cooking more, in general," said another.

Each time I arrived at a friend's house and there were pots simmering on the stove, many bottles of wine and local beer chilling, I tended to forget about the weather. The gray world suddenly smelled like sweet, earthy winter onions, simmering chicken, chiles and mushrooms.

One of the rituals we developed at our swaps was to share a story about the inspiration for the soup we brought. Some of these stories involved finding a special ingredient at a winter farmers' market, or discovering a new recipe on our travels. But the majority of the soups, and the stories that went along with them, had to do with family traditions and nostalgia.

Much has been written about soup as comfort food (its healing properties are undisputed), but there's also no denying soup's ability to evoke powerful memories: the Campbell's tomato soup and grilled cheese sandwiches that my mother served up; the rich bread-and-cheese-crowned French onion soup I tasted on my first trip to France; and the matzo ball soup with fresh dill my mother-in-law taught me to cook for Passover were some of what inspired me. And, of course, there were the soups I made for my own daughters when they were young and craved the salty canned variety their friends were eating. Slowly, over time, they took to loving their mother's homemade versions.

After a year of trading soups, recipes and stories with friends, I decided to write a book about this tradition. *Soup Swap* (Chronicle Books) is more than a collection of favorite recipes; it's also a guide to throwing your own party and learning how to build community—whether with neighbors, family or your book club.

At the end of every gathering, when I braved the elements to return home with my stash—a Turkish vegetable soup with lamb and beef meatballs, a roasted pumpkin soup for lunch the next day and a hearty cauliflower soup for dinner the day after that (not to mention a freezer filled with the others)—I knew I had meals to last all week, but so much more.

I like to think that soup is capable of more than just sustenance; it also feeds your soul. Sharing soup with friends and neighbors, and going home with the leftovers, is like taking home bowls of friendship and comfort, nutrition and warmth.

KATHY GUNST is a James Beard Award–winning writer and regular contributor to NPR. She lives and swaps soups in South Berwick, Maine.

TIPS FOR HOSTING

There's no one right way to throw a swap, but it does pay to think through how you want the whole thing to go down and to lay out some guidelines for your party.

Want everyone to taste all of the soups at the party?
Yes. Then everyone should bring enough to share that night and a pot to heat it in. Plus they will also need to bring some soup (ideally separately, and already packaged) to send home with each guest. This approach can be tricky if you have lots of people and just one stove to heat all the soups. So it's better for smaller groups, say 6 or fewer.
No. Then everyone just brings their soup already packaged and labeled to send home with each guest. If this is the case, we suggest that the host serves their own soup on the night of the party, plus some salad, bread and cheese to go with it.

Do you have enough bowls and spoons for everyone? Mugs or ramekins make good stand-ins, especially if you're just having a small taste of each batch. They don't need to match. Wash spoons as you taste, if needed. And, if you're serving a bunch of different soups to taste the night of the party, have each person bring their own ladle with their name on it.

How much to make? We like to send everyone home with about one quart (4 cups) of each soup. So the totals depend on how many people are coming to the swap—a little math may be in order. Most of the recipes in this chapter make 12 to 16 cups— enough for 3 or 4 people.

Who makes what? If you want to make sure there's a nice balance of soups, let everyone sign up in a Google doc or use plain old email. Don't forget dietary restrictions; you'll need to plan for those.

Make tags. Between sips of soup and wine, arm your friends with paper, markers and ribbons so they can craft labels.

ROASTED CAULIFLOWER SOUP WITH PARSLEY-CHIVE SWIRL

Blitzed cauliflower gives this very easy soup its dairy-free but creamy taste. To get the silkiest texture, puree the soup in a blender rather than using an immersion blender.

5 pounds cauliflower, cut into 1-inch florets (about 18 cups)

2 large leeks, white and pale green parts only, halved lengthwise, rinsed and cut into ½-inch pieces *(see Tip, page 197)*

1½ cups extra-virgin olive oil, divided

1¾ teaspoons kosher salt, divided

1¾ teaspoons ground pepper, divided

2½ cups fresh parsley

⅔ cup fresh chives

12 cups low-sodium "no-chicken" *or* chicken broth

5 teaspoons white-wine vinegar

1. Preheat oven to 400°F. Coat 2 large rimmed baking sheets with cooking spray.

2. Toss cauliflower and leeks with ½ cup oil and 1¼ teaspoons each salt and pepper in a very large bowl (you may need to do this in 2 batches). Divide the vegetables evenly between the prepared baking sheets. Roast, switching the pans from top to bottom and back to front halfway, until soft and browned on the bottom, 25 to 30 minutes.

3. Meanwhile, place parsley, chives and the remaining ½ teaspoon each salt and pepper in a blender; pulse several times to chop, scraping down the sides once or twice. With the motor running, slowly add the remaining 1 cup oil and process until smooth. Transfer the sauce to a bowl and rinse out the blender.

4. Transfer the roasted vegetables to a large pot and add broth. Bring to a boil over high heat. Reduce heat, cover and simmer for 10 minutes. Puree the soup in batches in a blender. (Use caution when blending hot liquids.) Stir in vinegar. Serve with some of the herb sauce swirled on top.

▸▸ **MAKE AHEAD:** Refrigerate for up to 3 days or freeze for up to 3 months.

SERVES 12: 1½ CUPS SOUP & GENEROUS 1 TBSP. SAUCE EACH

Calories 329 | Fat 29g (sat 4g) | Cholesterol 0mg | Carbs 16g | Total sugars 6g (added 0g) | Protein 4g | Fiber 4g | Sodium 482mg | Potassium 621mg.
Nutrition bonus: Vitamin C (166 daily value) | Vitamin A (35% dv) | Folate (34% dv) .

ROASTED PUMPKIN SOUP WITH GLAZED PEPITAS

You'll need a pie pumpkin (also called sugar pumpkin), not the carving kind, for this recipe. Look for ones between 4 and 8 pounds. Roasting brings out a sweet, almost smoky flavor and creates a soup with depth and character. Plain pepitas are a good topper, but the homemade glazed ones here are really special.

EQUIPMENT: PARCHMENT PAPER

- 1 7-pound pie pumpkin *or* winter squash, peeled, seeded and cut into 1-inch pieces (about 18 cups)
- 2 medium onions, thinly sliced
- ⅓ cup extra-virgin olive oil plus 1 tablespoon, divided
- 4 tablespoons chopped fresh sage, divided
- 4 tablespoons chopped fresh thyme, divided
- 2¼ teaspoons kosher salt, divided
- 1 teaspoon ground pepper plus a pinch, divided
- ⅔ cup dry white wine
- ¾ cup pepitas
- 3 tablespoons maple syrup
- 8 cups low-sodium "no-chicken" broth
- 1 cup water

1. Position racks in upper and lower thirds of oven; preheat to 450°F. Coat 2 large rimmed baking sheets with cooking spray.

2. Toss pumpkin (or squash) and onions with ⅓ cup oil, 3 tablespoons each sage and thyme and 1 teaspoon each salt and pepper in a very large bowl (you may need to do this in 2 batches). Divide between the prepared baking sheets. Roast, stirring once halfway and switching the pans from top to bottom and back to front, until lightly browned and tender, 25 to 30 minutes. Remove from the oven and immediately add ⅓ cup wine to each pan, scraping up any browned bits.

3. Meanwhile, heat the remaining 1 tablespoon oil in a small skillet over medium heat. Add pepitas, ¼ teaspoon salt and the remaining pinch of pepper; cook, stirring, until toasted, 2 to 4 minutes. Add maple syrup and cook, stirring, until well coated and lightly caramelized, 1 to 3 minutes more. Spread on a parchment-lined plate to cool.

4. Transfer the vegetables and any accumulated juices to a large stockpot and add broth and water. Stir in the remaining 1 tablespoon each sage and thyme and 1 teaspoon salt. Cover and bring to a boil over high heat. Reduce heat, partially cover and simmer for 15 minutes.

5. Puree the soup with an immersion blender or in batches in a regular blender. (Use caution when blending hot liquids.) Serve the soup topped with the glazed pepitas.

▶▶ **MAKE AHEAD:** Refrigerate soup for up to 3 days or freeze for up to 3 months. Store glazed pepitas at room temperature for up to 3 days.

SERVES 12: 1½ CUPS SOUP & 1 TBSP. PEPITAS EACH

Calories 194 | Fat 11g (sat 2g) | Cholesterol 0mg | Carbs 19g | Total sugars 9g (added 3g) | Protein 4g | Fiber 2g | Sodium 475mg | Potassium 649mg.
Nutrition bonus: Vitamin A (297% daily value) | Vitamin C (31% dv).

POTATO-LEEK BISQUE

Croutons topped with anchovy, olives and leek are a crunchy, savory foil to this rich and creamy soup. But skip them if you like and incorporate all the cooked leeks into the soup instead.

SOUP

- 3 tablespoons extra-virgin olive oil
- 4½ pounds leeks, white and light green parts only, sliced (*see Tip*)
- ¾ teaspoon salt, divided
- 2¼ pounds Yukon Gold potatoes, peeled and diced
- 4½ cups nonfat *or* low-fat milk
- 3 cups low-sodium chicken broth
- ¼ cup lemon juice
- ¼ teaspoon ground white pepper, or to taste
  Thinly sliced fresh chives for garnish

CROUTONS

- ½ cup minced pitted oil-cured olives
- 4 anchovies, minced
- ¼ teaspoon ground pepper
- 12 slices baguette, preferably whole-wheat, toasted

1. To prepare bisque: Heat oil in a large pot over medium heat. Add leeks and ¼ teaspoon salt. Cook, stirring occasionally, until very tender but not brown, 20 to 30 minutes. Adjust heat as necessary and add a bit of water if needed to prevent sticking. Set aside ⅔ cup of the leeks in a small bowl.

2. Add potatoes, milk and broth to the pot. Bring to a simmer (do not boil) and cook, stirring occasionally, until the potatoes are very tender, 10 to 15 minutes.

3. To prepare croutons: Meanwhile, add olives, anchovies and black pepper to the reserved leeks; mix well. Divide evenly among the toasted baguette slices.

4. When the potatoes are tender, remove from the heat. Puree the soup with an immersion blender or in batches in a regular blender. (Use caution when blending hot liquids.) Season with the remaining ½ teaspoon salt, lemon juice and white pepper. Divide among 12 soup bowls and float a crouton on top of each. Garnish with chives, if desired.

▸▸ **MAKE AHEAD:** Refrigerate bisque and crouton toppings separately for up to 3 days.

SERVES 12: ABOUT 1 CUP SOUP & 1 CROUTON EACH

Calories 275 | Fat 7g (sat 1g) | Cholesterol 3mg | Carbs 46g | Total sugars 8g (added 0g) | Protein 9g | Fiber 3g | Sodium 566mg | Potassium 589mg.
Nutrition bonus: Vitamin C (30% daily value) | Vitamin A (28% dv).

Clean leeks well to be sure they're grit-free: After slicing, swish around in a bowl of water to release any sand or soil trapped between the layers. Scoop the leeks out of the bowl with a slotted spoon, leaving any sand or soil behind in the bowl. Drain well. Repeat as needed.

QUINOA MUSHROOM SOUP

Reminiscent of old-fashioned mushroom barley, this soup gets a modern update with nutrient-packed quinoa.

1½ ounces dried porcini mushrooms

2½ cups boiling water

5 tablespoons extra-virgin olive oil, divided

2¼ pounds mixed mushrooms, thinly sliced

¼ teaspoon ground pepper

¾ cup dry sherry *or* dry vermouth

3 large onions, finely chopped

6 stalks celery, chopped

3 large carrots, halved lengthwise and thinly sliced

1 large red bell pepper, chopped

12 cups mushroom broth *or* low-sodium chicken broth

1 15-ounce can no-salt-added crushed tomatoes *or* tomato puree

1½ cups quinoa

3 tablespoons dried marjoram *or* oregano

3 bay leaves

2 tablespoons reduced-sodium tamari *or* soy sauce

1. Place porcini in a small bowl; add boiling water, cover and let stand for 20 minutes.

2. Meanwhile, heat 3 tablespoons oil in a stockpot over medium-high heat. Add fresh mushrooms, sprinkle with pepper and cook without stirring for 2 minutes. Stir and continue to cook, stirring once or twice, until the mushrooms have given off their liquid and are well browned, about 10 minutes more. Add sherry (or vermouth) and cook, stirring, for 1 minute.

3. Add the remaining 2 tablespoons oil to the pot along with onions, celery, carrots and bell pepper and cook, stirring frequently, until the onions are tender and translucent, about 15 minutes.

4. Line a sieve with a paper towel, place over a bowl and strain the porcini; reserve the liquid. Chop the porcini and add to the pot along with the strained liquid. Add broth, tomatoes, quinoa, marjoram (or oregano) and bay leaves; bring to a boil. Reduce heat to a simmer, cover and cook for 20 minutes. Remove from heat and stir in tamari (or soy sauce).

SERVES 12: 2 CUPS EACH

Calories 186 | Fat 7g (sat 1g) | Cholesterol 0mg | Carbs 23g | Total sugars 6g (added 0g) | Protein 6g | Fiber 5g | Sodium 600mg | Potassium 670mg.
Nutrition bonus: Vitamin A (72% daily value) | Vitamin C (24% dv).

NEW MEXICO GREEN CHILE AND PORK STEW

Three types of chiles, both fresh and canned, bring different kinds of heat, earthiness and sweetness to this stew. If you can get Hatch chiles, by all means use them. Pepper aficionados love them so much they travel in droves to a New Mexico festival celebrating their fall harvest.

3 poblano peppers *or* Hatch chiles

4 tablespoons safflower oil, divided

5 pounds boneless pork shoulder, trimmed well and cut into 1-inch cubes

3 teaspoons kosher salt, divided

1 teaspoon ground pepper

3 large onions, finely chopped

5 cloves garlic, finely chopped

2 4½-ounce cans chopped roasted green chiles

2-4 tablespoons chopped jalapeño pepper, seeded if desired

1½ tablespoons dried oregano, preferably Mexican

2 bay leaves

4 cups low-sodium chicken broth *or* beef broth

4 cups water

1½ pounds potatoes, peeled and cut into ½-inch pieces

¾ cup chopped fresh cilantro, divided

1. Char peppers (or chiles) directly over a gas flame, flipping them over from time to time so they blacken on all sides, 4 to 5 minutes total. *(Alternatively, preheat broiler to high. Place peppers on a baking sheet and broil, turning occasionally, until the skin blisters, 6 to 10 minutes total.)* Transfer to a medium bowl, cover with plastic wrap and let steam for 5 minutes to loosen the skins. Remove and discard skin, core and seeds and coarsely chop the flesh. Set aside.

2. Heat 2 tablespoons oil in a large stockpot over medium-high heat. Season pork with 1½ teaspoons salt and pepper. Cook half the pork until browned on all sides, about 5 minutes. Transfer to a bowl. Repeat with 1 tablespoon oil and the remaining pork; transfer to the bowl.

3. Reduce heat to medium and add the remaining 1 tablespoon oil, onions and garlic; cook, stirring occasionally, until soft, about 5 minutes. Add the reserved peppers, canned chiles and jalapeño to taste; cook, stirring occasionally, for 5 minutes. Return the pork to the pot and add oregano, bay leaves, broth and water; bring to a boil. Reduce heat to low, partially cover and cook until the pork is just about fork-tender, 1¼ to 1½ hours.

4. Add potatoes and ½ cup cilantro; cover and cook over low heat until the potatoes are tender, 20 to 30 minutes more. Skim the fat from the top of the soup, if desired. Stir in the remaining 1½ teaspoons salt. Serve topped with the remaining ¼ cup cilantro.

▸▸ **MAKE AHEAD:** Refrigerate for up to 3 days or freeze for up to 3 months.

SERVES 14: 1½ CUPS EACH

Calories 380 | Fat 22g (sat 7g) | Cholesterol 99mg | Carbs 16g | Total sugars 3g (added 0g) | Protein 28g | Fiber 2g | Sodium 570mg | Potassium 614mg. Nutrition bonus: Vitamin C (60% daily value).

MATZO BALL SOUP WITH FRESH DILL

The secret to light, fluffy matzo balls is twofold: use seltzer instead of tap water and let the mixture rest in the refrigerator so it's fully hydrated before cooking. The vegetables can be finely sliced to make an elegant soup or coarsely chopped or sliced for a more rustic presentation.

MATZO BALLS

- 6 large eggs
- 6 tablespoons canola oil
- 1½ cups whole-wheat matzo meal
- ½ cup seltzer
- 1½ tablespoons minced fresh dill
- 1 teaspoon kosher salt
- ½ teaspoon ground pepper

SOUP

- 6 pounds bone-in chicken pieces
- 6 medium carrots, very thinly sliced
- 4 stalks celery, very thinly sliced
- 3 medium onions, halved and very thinly sliced
- 3 small parsnips, peeled and very thinly sliced
- 6 whole black peppercorns
- 2 bay leaves
- 2 teaspoons kosher salt
- 14 cups water
- ½ cup chopped fresh parsley plus 6 tablespoons, divided
- 6 tablespoons chopped fresh dill, divided

1. To prepare matzo balls: Whisk eggs in a large bowl. Add oil and whisk to combine. Add matzo meal, seltzer, minced dill, 1 teaspoon salt and pepper; mix until combined. Cover and refrigerate for at least 2 hours and up to 6 hours.

2. Meanwhile, to prepare soup: Place chicken, carrots, celery, onions, parsnips, peppercorns, bay leaves and salt in a large stockpot; add water. Bring to a boil over high heat, skimming any foam that rises to the surface. Reduce heat to low and add ½ cup parsley and 3 tablespoons dill. Partially cover and simmer for 1¼ hours.

3. Transfer the chicken to a large bowl and let cool. Skim fat off the soup, if desired.

4. While the chicken cools, bring a large pot of water to a boil over high heat. With wet hands and using a generous 2 tablespoons for each, form the matzo mixture into 16 balls about 2 inches in diameter. Add the matzo balls to the boiling water; return to a boil, then reduce heat to medium-low. Cover and cook for 25 minutes.

5. Remove the chicken from the bones. (Discard skin and bones.) Shred the chicken and stir into the soup.

6. Using a slotted spoon, transfer the cooked matzo balls to the soup. Return the soup to a simmer over medium heat. Combine in a small bowl the remaining 6 tablespoons parsley and 3 tablespoons dill. Serve the soup sprinkled with the herbs.

▶▶ **MAKE AHEAD:** Refrigerate soup with matzo balls for up to 3 days. Freeze soup and matzo balls separately for up to 3 months.

SERVES 16: 1½ CUPS SOUP & 1 MATZO BALL EACH

Calories 278 | Fat 12g (sat 2g) | Cholesterol 157mg | Carbs 15g | Total sugars 3g (added 0g) | Protein 25g | Fiber 3g | Sodium 490mg | Potassium 416mg.
Nutrition bonus: Vitamin A (86% daily value).

CHICKEN, BARLEY AND MUSHROOM SOUP

This soup is chock-full of sturdy root vegetables and whole-grain barley. You can use any combination of dried and fresh mushrooms here. The soup will thicken as it sits on the stove— thin it as needed with more broth or water.

1 ounce dried shiitake mushrooms

2 cups boiling water

2 tablespoons extra-virgin olive oil

3 medium leeks, white and light green parts only, washed and coarsely chopped (see Tip, page 197)

3 cloves garlic, chopped

2 medium carrots, chopped

8 ounces fresh shiitake mushrooms, stems removed, caps coarsely chopped

8 ounces white mushrooms, sliced

1 teaspoon salt

Coarsely ground pepper to taste

1 pound boneless, skinless chicken thighs, trimmed and cut into ¼-inch pieces

6 cups low-sodium chicken broth

½ cup pearl barley

1 tablespoon minced fresh thyme or 1 teaspoon dried

1 teaspoon sherry vinegar

1. Soak dried shiitakes in boiling water for 20 minutes. Strain through a fine-mesh sieve and reserve the liquid. Squeeze the mushrooms to remove excess liquid, then dice.

2. Meanwhile, heat oil in a large pot over medium heat. Add leeks and garlic; cook, stirring, until very soft, about 4 minutes. Add carrots, fresh shiitakes, white mushrooms, salt and pepper; cook, stirring, until the vegetables start to soften, 3 to 4 minutes. Add chicken and cook, stirring, until it is no longer pink on the outside, about 4 minutes.

3. Add broth, barley, thyme, the reserved soaking liquid and the chopped soaked mushrooms. Increase heat to high and bring to a simmer. Reduce heat to medium-low, partially cover and simmer until the barley is tender, about 50 minutes. Stir in vinegar.

SERVES 8: 1¼ CUPS EACH

Calories 241 | Fat 9g (sat 2g) | Cholesterol 38mg | Carbs 24g | Total sugars 4g (added 0g) | Protein 18g | Fiber 4g | Sodium 401mg | Potassium 611mg.
Nutrition bonus: Vitamin A (63% daily value).

WINTER VEGETABLE SOUP WITH TURKISH MEATBALLS

The warming spices in these meatballs make this soup perfect for sub-zero nights.

SOUP

- 3 tablespoons extra-virgin olive oil
- 2 medium leeks, white and pale green parts only, halved lengthwise, rinsed and sliced (see Tip, page 197)
- 3 medium onions, coarsely chopped
- 5 cloves garlic, chopped
- 6 medium carrots, thinly sliced
- 4 stalks celery, thinly sliced
- 3 medium parsnips, peeled and thinly sliced
- 1½ teaspoons kosher salt
- 1 teaspoon ground pepper
- 1 pound potatoes, cut into ½-inch pieces
- 1½ cups canned crushed tomatoes
- 1½ tablespoons chopped fresh thyme
- 8 cups low-sodium chicken broth

MEATBALLS & GARNISH

- ¼ cup extra-virgin olive oil, divided
- 1 medium onion, finely chopped
- 1 scallion, finely chopped
- 2 small cloves garlic, minced
- 1 cup finely chopped fresh mint, divided
- ¾ teaspoon kosher salt
- ¾ teaspoon ground pepper
- ¾ teaspoon ground cinnamon, divided
- ¾ teaspoon ground cumin, divided
- 1¼ pounds lean ground beef and/or lamb
- ¾ cup whole-wheat panko breadcrumbs
- 1 large egg plus 1 large egg white, beaten
- 1½ cups whole-milk Greek yogurt

1. To prepare soup: Heat 3 tablespoons oil in a large stockpot over medium heat. Add leeks, 3 onions and 5 garlic cloves; cook, stirring occasionally, until soft but not brown, about 10 minutes. Add carrots, celery, parsnips, 1½ teaspoons salt and 1 teaspoon pepper; cook, stirring occasionally, for 3 minutes. Stir in potatoes. Increase heat to high and add tomatoes and thyme; cook, stirring occasionally, for 2 minutes. Add broth and bring to a boil. Reduce heat, partially cover and simmer for 20 minutes.

2. Meanwhile, prepare meatballs: Heat 2 tablespoons oil in a large skillet over medium heat. Add onion, scallion and garlic; cook, stirring, for 5 minutes. Add 2 tablespoons mint, salt, pepper and ½ teaspoon each cinnamon and cumin; cook, stirring, for 1 minute. Scrape into a large bowl and let cool slightly. Wash and dry the pan.

3. Add beef (and/or lamb), panko, eggs, 2 table-spoons mint and the remaining ¼ teaspoon each cinnamon and cumin to the onion mixture; mix. Using a generous 1 tablespoon, form into 28 meatballs.

4. Heat 1 tablespoon oil in the pan over medium-high heat. Reduce heat to medium and add half the meatballs. Cook, turning occasionally, until browned on all sides but not cooked through, 6 to 8 minutes. Transfer to the soup. Repeat with remaining 1 table-spoon oil and meatballs. Simmer soup until meatballs are cooked through, about 15 minutes. Serve the soup topped with yogurt and remaining ¾ cup mint.

SERVES 14: 1½ CUPS EACH

Calories 296 | Fat 14g (sat 4g) | Cholesterol 43mg | Carbs 27g | Total sugars 7g (added 0g) | Protein 17g | Fiber 5g | Sodium 485mg | Potassium 791mg.
Nutrition bonus: Vitamin A (102% daily value) | Vitamin C (28% dv) | Iron (22% dv) | Vitamin B_{12} (21% dv).

SOUPS BY THE FORMULA

There is no food that is more adaptable than soup. Its very essence is amalgamation—a delicious jumbling up of various vegetables, proteins, herbs and seasonings. These formulas for three favorites—chicken soup, chowder and pureed vegetable soup—let you learn the basic steps and then customize your soup exactly to your liking.

CLASSIC
CHICKEN SOUP
P.213

ACTIVE 40 MIN
TOTAL 1 HR

CHANGEABLE CHICKEN SOUP

Every pot starts with garlic, onions, bone-in chicken breast and low-sodium broth. From there, make it your own with seasonings, vegetables, grains and/or beans. (*Variations: pages 212-213.*)

1. LAY THE BASE Heat 2 Tbsp. extra-virgin **olive oil** in a large pot over medium heat; add 1 cup chopped **onion** and 2 minced **garlic** cloves. Cook, stirring, until softened, 2 to 3 minutes. Add 2 to 4 tsp. **seasonings** total (*see below*). Cook, stirring, 1 to 2 minutes more.

DRIED
• bay leaf
• marjoram
• oregano
• rosemary
• sage
• thyme

GROUND
• allspice
• cayenne
• chili powder
• chipotle
• cinnamon
• coriander
• cumin

• curry powder
• paprika

MINCED
• chipotle chiles in adobo
• ginger
• lemongrass

2. HACK "HOMEMADE" BROTH Save time by using boxed or canned broth. Make it taste homemade by cooking the chicken for the soup in the broth before adding other ingredients. Pour 8 cups **low-sodium chicken broth** into the pot with the seasonings. Add 2 lb. **bone-in chicken breasts** (without skin); simmer until cooked through (165°F on an instant-read thermometer), 20 to 22 minutes. While it cooks, skim any foam from the surface to keep the broth clear. Transfer the chicken to a clean cutting board to cool, then shred into bite-size pieces.

3. LOAD IT WITH VEGETABLES Add 6 to 8 cups **vegetables** (fresh or frozen, thawed) to the broth after you take out the chicken. Return to a simmer; cook until the vegetables are tender, 4 to 10 minutes.

CHOPPED
• bell pepper
• broccoli
• cauliflower
• celeriac
• dark leafy greens
• green beans
• potatoes
• rutabaga

• sweet potatoes
• tomatoes
• turnip
• winter squash

SLICED
• cabbage
• carrots
• celery

• fennel
• mushrooms
• zucchini or summer squash

WHOLE
• corn kernels
• peas

4. BUMP UP FIBER Add 3 cups cooked **pasta,** whole **grains** or 1½ cups cooked **beans** (or one 15-oz. can beans, rinsed) to the pot. Stir in the chicken, 1¼ tsp. **salt** and ½ tsp. **pepper.** Cook until heated through.

PASTA (whole-wheat)
• egg noodles
• fusilli
• macaroni
• orzo
• spaghetti
• udon

GRAINS
• barley
• brown rice
• farro
• freekeh
• millet
• quinoa
• wheat berries

BEANS
• black beans
• cannellini or navy beans
• chickpeas
• kidney beans

5. GO FOR BIG FLAVOR Just before serving, add one more layer with a **flavor burst**—it can be something as simple as parsley or lime juice. For a more complex finish, stir in pesto or chile paste.

FRESH HERBS (1-4 Tbsp.)
• basil
• chives
• cilantro
• dill
• mint
• parsley
• tarragon

HERB SAUCES (2-4 Tbsp.)
• chimichurri
• pesto
• salsa verde

HOT SAUCES (1-3 tsp.)
• chile-garlic
• curry paste
• harissa
• Sriracha

ACID (1-3 Tbsp.)
• lemon juice
• lime juice
• vinegar

UMAMI (1-3 Tbsp.)
• fish sauce
• miso
• reduced-sodium soy sauce or tamari

➤ **MAKE AHEAD:** Refrigerate (without pasta or grains, if using, and without flavor burst), for up to 3 days. To serve, stir in pasta or grains and reheat, then stir in flavor burst.

SERVES 8: 1½ CUPS EACH

JAPANESE CHICKEN NOODLE

SEASONINGS:
1 Tbsp. minced fresh ginger

VEGETABLES:
3 cups sliced green cabbage, 2 cups sliced shiitake mushroom caps, 2 cups thinly sliced carrots

PASTA:
3 cups cooked udon noodles *or* whole-wheat spaghetti

FLAVOR BOOST:
2 Tbsp. white miso

CHICKEN SOUP 5 WAYS

Whether you go for the chicken noodle or have a taste for fiery Moroccan-inspired soup, we've got you covered. Follow the Changeable Chicken Soup master recipe on page 211 and choose one of these variations—or make up your own!

PESTO CHICKEN & CANNELLINI BEAN

SEASONINGS:
1 tsp. dried marjoram, 1 tsp. dried oregano

VEGETABLES:
3 cups sliced fennel, 3 cups chopped broccolini (1-inch pieces), 2 cups chopped fresh tomatoes

BEANS:
15-oz. can cannellini beans, rinsed

FLAVOR BOOST:
¼ cup pesto

CLASSIC

SEASONINGS:
1 tsp. dried thyme,
1 bay leaf

VEGETABLES:
2 cups each sliced
celery, sliced carrots
& frozen peas

PASTA:
3 cups cooked
whole-wheat
egg noodles

FLAVOR BOOST:
¼ cup chopped
fresh parsley

CHIPOTLE CHICKEN & VEGETABLE

SEASONINGS:
2 tsp. finely chopped
chipotle chiles in
adobo (*or* 1 tsp.
ground chipotle),
1½ tsp. ground
cumin, ¼ tsp. allspice

VEGETABLES:
3 cups corn kernels,
2 cups sliced zucchini,
2 cups halved
cherry tomatoes

GRAINS:
3 cups cooked
brown rice

FLAVOR BOOST:
2-3 Tbsp.
lime juice

MOROCCAN CHICKEN & SWEET POTATO

SEASONINGS:
1½ tsp. ground
cumin, ½ tsp. ground
cinnamon, ¼ tsp.
cayenne

VEGETABLES:
3 cups diced sweet
potato, 2 cups diced
bell pepper, 2 cups
green beans
(2-inch pieces)

BEANS:
15-oz. can
chickpeas, rinsed

FLAVOR BOOST:
1 tsp. harissa,
or to taste

MAKE-AHEAD
Refrigerate cooked
noodles or grains
separately from
the rest of the soup
and add them just
before serving.

CHOOSE A CHOWDER

We've simmered our favorite technique for making creamy, comforting chowder into 5 simple steps. Every pot starts with onion, celery, flour, broth, and milk. Choose herbs, spices, vegetables, proteins and garnishes to create your own variation. *(See variations on pages 216-217.)*

1. LAY THE BASE The best chowders start with a combination of aromatic vegetables cooked in oil to bring out their flavor. To start, heat 3 tablespoons extra-virgin **olive oil** in a large pot over medium heat; add 1 cup each diced **onion** and **celery**. Cook, stirring frequently, until softened and beginning to brown, 3 to 6 minutes. Sprinkle ½ cup **flour**, ¼ teaspoon **salt** and ¼ teaspoon to 1 tablespoon **seasonings** over the vegetables and cook, stirring, for 1 minute more.

- bay leaf
- chili powder
- cumin
- dry mustard
- marjoram
- Old Bay
- oregano
- pepper
- thyme
- Worcestershire sauce

2. ADD BROTH Save time by using boxed or canned broth. Pour 4 cups **broth** or stock and 1 cup **whole milk** into the pot. Bring to a gentle boil, stirring constantly.

- reduced- or low-sodium chicken broth
- reduced-sodium vegetable broth
- "no-chicken" broth
- fish or seafood stock
- clam juice

3. LOAD IT WITH VEGETABLES Add 3 to 6 cups **vegetables** to the pot and bring just to a simmer. Simmer, uncovered, stirring occasionally, until the vegetables are tender, 12 to 15 minutes.

CHOPPED
- broccoli
- carrots
- cauliflower
- green beans
- peppers
- potatoes
- yellow squash *or* zucchini
- sweet potatoes

WHOLE
- corn kernels
- peas

4. PUMP UP THE PROTEIN Depending on the variation you're making, add one of the following after the vegetables are tender and simmer, stirring frequently, until cooked and/or heated through, 2 to 6 minutes.

- 1 lb. boneless, skinless **chicken breast** *or* **cod**, cut into 1-inch pieces
- 1 cup shredded **Cheddar cheese**
- 16 oz. chopped fresh **clams** (liquid reserved)
- ¾ cup diced **ham** steak
- 2 cans (15 oz.) **black beans,** rinsed

5. GARNISH IT Top with the garnishes of your choice.

- diced **onion** *or* **tomato**
- crumbled cooked **bacon**
- shredded **cheese**
- fresh **herbs** *or* **scallions**
- toasted **nuts** *or* **seeds**
- **lime wedges**

▸▸ **MAKE AHEAD:** Refrigerate for up to 3 days. To serve, slowly reheat over medium-low or microwave on Medium.

SERVES 6: ABOUT 1½ CUPS EACH

ALASKAN COD
CHOWDER
P. 216

BROCCOLI-CHEDDAR-CHICKEN

SEASONINGS:
1 tsp. dry mustard,
¼ tsp. ground pepper

BROTH/STOCK:
4 cups low-sodium
chicken broth

VEGETABLES:
2 cups diced Yukon
Gold potatoes,
3 cups chopped
broccoli

PROTEIN:
1 lb. boneless,
skinless chicken
breast, 1 cup
shredded Cheddar
cheese

GARNISHES:
Diced red onion,
shredded Cheddar
cheese

ALASKAN COD

SEASONINGS:
1 Tbsp Worcestershire
sauce, ¾ tsp.
reduced-sodium
Old Bay seasoning,
¼ tsp. ground pepper

BROTH/STOCK:
4 cups fish or
seafood stock

VEGETABLES:
3 cups diced red
potatoes, 2 cups
chopped green beans

PROTEIN:
1 lb. Alaskan cod,
cut into 1-inch pieces

GARNISHES:
Snipped fresh dill,
diced plum tomatoes

SQUASH & CORN

SEASONINGS:
1¼ tsp. dried
marjoram, ¼ tsp.
ground pepper

BROTH/STOCK:
4 cups low-sodium
chicken broth

VEGETABLES:
2 cups diced yellow
squash, 2 cups diced
red potatoes, 1 cup
corn kernels

PROTEIN:
¾ cup diced
ham steak

GARNISHES:
Sliced scallions,
shredded pepper
Jack cheese

CHOWDER 5 WAYS

When you make your own chowder you can save 300 calories, 20 grams of saturated fat and 500 milligrams of sodium per serving compared to many store-bought or restaurant chowders.

CLAM

SEASONINGS:
½ tsp. dried thyme, ¼ tsp. ground pepper, 1 bay leaf

BROTH/STOCK:
4 cups clam juice

VEGETABLES:
3 cups diced white potatoes

PROTEIN:
16-oz. chopped fresh clams (plus their liquid), thawed if frozen

GARNISHES:
Chopped cooked bacon, snipped chives

SOUTHWESTERN VEGETABLE

SEASONINGS:
1 Tbsp. chili powder, 1½ tsp. ground cumin, 1 tsp. dried oregano

BROTH/STOCK:
4 cups reduced-sodium vegetable broth

VEGETABLES:
2 cups diced sweet potatoes, 2 diced poblano or green bell peppers

PROTEIN:
Two 15-oz. cans black beans, rinsed

GARNISHES:
Chopped cilantro, toasted pepitas, lime wedges

PUREED VEGETABLE SOUP

Too many carrots? Broccoli starting to soften? Want to celebrate the first spring peas? Turn them into a silky-smooth soup. They all shine here and, once you master this easy method, you can use it for any vegetable you like—try cauliflower, butternut squash, parsnips or celery root. Serve these whipped-up soups as starters or enjoy one with a salad and crusty bread for a simple meal.

1. LAY THE BASE The best soups start with a combination of aromatic vegetables cooked in oil to bring out their flavor. The difference here is that we add some butter too for extra flavor. To start, heat 1 Tbsp. each **butter** and **olive oil** in a large pot over medium heat until the butter melts. Add 1 chopped medium **onion** and 1 chopped **celery** stalk. Cook, stirring occasionally, until softened, 4 to 6 minutes. Add 2 chopped **garlic** cloves and 1 tsp. chopped fresh **thyme** *or* **parsley** and cook, stirring, until fragrant, about 10 seconds.

2. CHOOSE YOUR VEGETABLE You can pick almost anything here. Keep all the pieces the same size so they cook evenly. Add the **vegetables** to the pot and then pour in the liquid: 4 cups **low-sodium chicken broth** diluted with some water to keep the sodium in check. (Water amounts are listed with the combinations, *opposite.*)

- peeled potatoes, rutabaga, sweet potatoes, squash *or* turnips
- broccoli *or* cauliflower
- carrots
- peas *or* asparagus

3. COOK UNTIL TENDER Bring the soup to a lively simmer over high heat. Reduce heat to maintain a lively simmer and cook until the vegetables are very tender *(see cooking times, opposite).*

4. MAKE IT SMOOTH Puree the soup with an immersion blender or in batches in a blender until smooth. (Use caution when blending hot liquids.) Stir in ½ cup **half-and-half** for a little extra richness, if desired *(see Tip)*, and ½ tsp. **salt** and **pepper** to taste.

Adding a splash of half-and-half adds richness to these creamy soups, but without it, the flavor of the featured vegetable is more intense.

➤➤ **MAKE AHEAD:** Refrigerate for up to 4 days or freeze for up to 3 months.

SERVES 8: ABOUT 1 CUP EACH

POTATO SOUP

STEP 2:
5 cups chopped
peeled potatoes
2 cups water
STEP 3:
Simmer for about 15 minutes.

BROCCOLI SOUP

STEP 2:
8 cups chopped broccoli
(stems and florets)
2 cups water
STEP 3:
Simmer for about 8 minutes.

CARROT SOUP

STEP 2:
5 cups chopped
carrots
2 cups water
STEP 3:
Simmer for about 25 minutes.

PEA SOUP

STEP 2:
6 cups peas
(fresh or frozen)
½ cup water
STEP 3:
Simmer for 1 minute.

TOP IT OFF

Think of what the cherry does for a sundae—it adds a bit of flavor and a dash of good looks. Before you dip your spoon into your bowl of soup, sprinkle, drizzle, swirl or squeeze a little extra beauty on top with creative toppers. Here's some inspiration, but really, these ideas are just a jumping-off point—anything goes!

SPRINKLES

Chopped herbs, such as chives, cilantro, dill *or* parsley

Dusting of spice, such as cumin, curry, paprika *or* white pepper

Lemon, lime *or* orange zest

Shaved, crumbled *or* grated cheese, such as feta, Parmesan *or* Pecorino

MORE VEGGIES!

Thinly sliced radish *or* cucumber

Julienned carrot, cabbage *or* jicama

Chopped tomato

Corn *or* peas

SWIRLS & DOLLOPS

Plain yogurt, sour cream *or* crème fraîche

Pesto, salsa, gremolata *or* caponata

Aioli *or* tzatziki

Extra-virgin olive oil, sesame oil, nut oil *or* any flavored oil, such as truffle

Hot sauce, such as Texas Pete *or* Sriracha

Hoisin sauce, fish sauce *or* soy sauce

Vinegar, such as sherry *or* red-wine

Lemon, lime *or* orange juice

CRUNCHIES

Croutons *or* toasted fresh breadcrumbs

Crumbled tortilla chips *or* crackers

Toasted nuts, such as almonds, pistachios *or* hazelnuts

Toasted pumpkin *or* sunflower seeds

Toasted coconut

SLOW-COOKER
CHICKEN STOCK
P.226

RESOURCES

There are some universally helpful things to know about soup-making: how to make broth, what ingredients to always keep on hand in your pantry and tips for the best way to freeze soups all rank up there as really good to know. This chapter gathers together some of the best tricks of the soup-making trade that you'll return to over and over.

STOCK (OR BROTH) UP!

Broth forms the base of most soups. We call for chicken, vegetable and "no-chicken" (a vegetarian one that tastes like chicken) most frequently because they're so versatile. Beef, mushroom and seafood broths are reserved for soups that benefit from their stronger flavors. In our recipes we assume many of you will use store-bought broth. Therefore in the ingredient lists we specify which broth to look for at the store. We've tested these recipes with that broth and our nutrition analysis reflects that choice. All that said, we know some of you will want to use homemade (it's delicious!) and we whole-heartedly encourage that. These recipes will all work with homemade broth, though you may have to adjust the added salt accordingly. (See Dan Duane's essay on page 230 if you want a little inspiration to start a batch of stock.) To keep all the broth (and stock!) terminology and labeling straight, here's a little primer:

Broth vs. stock: which is it?

We use these terms interchangeably. And you'll find them used that way on packaging as well. However, if you want to get serious, here's how many experts define them: stock and broth both contain a base of vegetables (carrots, celery, onions), herbs and water but "stock" is made with bones and "broth" with meat and no bones. As a stock simmers, collagen in the bones, cartilage and connective tissues breaks down, releasing gelatin and giving the stock a more viscous texture, especially when it's cooled.

Well, then what the heck is bone broth?

To make the terminology situation even more confusing, bone broth has come on the scene. It's made by simmering bones, along with vegetables and herbs, in water—so it's basically stock. Like stock, it has a bit more body than broth. The sodium level in store-bought bone broths varies, so read the labels.

What's up with bouillon paste?

Great to keep on hand for soup making, bouillon paste has a spoonable consistency that makes it easy to portion just the amount you need. To keep sodium in check, opt for reduced-sodium offerings.

Which one tastes best?

The most important thing is to find a broth or stock that pleases your palate. If you're inclined, try tasting a few side by side. You'll be surprised at how different they taste! Most store-bought broth is high in sodium, delivering close to 1,000 mg per cup. (The recommended daily cap for most adults is 2,300 mg.) Look for brands with less sodium that have these terms on the label:

- Reduced-sodium (averaging 500 mg/cup)
- No-salt-added (averaging 200 mg/cup)
- Low-sodium (140 mg or less/cup)

Some brands are lower in sodium, but not labeled as such—check the nutrition panel to compare. And remember, you can always add more salt if you want.

Got extra broth?

Extra broth will keep in the fridge for at least a week and for 6 months or more in the freezer. Here are some ways to use it up.

- Use instead of water to cook whole grains, such as brown rice, quinoa or barley.
- Moisten leftovers before reheating or use to make a savory bread pudding.
- Swap for water when steaming vegetables.
- Mash into potatoes instead of cream.
- Deglaze your pans—i.e., scrape up the browned bits—with broth instead of wine.
- Make gravy. Combine broth with flour or cornstarch, then whisk it into your pan drippings.

HOMEMADE ROASTED CHICKEN STOCK

This stock recipe starts with two leftover roasted chicken carcasses. If you don't have two ready at once, freeze one and save it until you roast another chicken. Simmering the bones with herbs and veggies makes a virtually sodium- and calorie-free broth that has a deep, delicious flavor.

EQUIPMENT: STOCKPOT

  2 roasted chicken carcasses (meat removed)
  1 cup chopped onion
  ¾ cup chopped carrot
  ¾ cup chopped celery
  6 cloves garlic
  6 sprigs fresh parsley
  3 sprigs fresh thyme
  1 bay leaf
 10 whole black peppercorns
 12 cups water

1. Place carcasses in a stockpot. Add onion, carrot, celery, garlic, parsley, thyme, bay leaf and peppercorns. Add water; bring to a boil. Reduce heat to maintain a gentle simmer; cook, uncovered, for 3 hours.

2. Remove from heat and let stand 30 minutes. Strain the stock through a fine-mesh sieve into a large bowl; discard the solids. If you have more than about 5 cups of stock, transfer it back to the pot and continue simmering until reduced to 5 cups.

➨ **MAKE AHEAD:** Refrigerate for up to 1 week or freeze for up to 3 months.

MAKES: 5 CUPS

Analysis note: After straining, stock has negligible calories, nutrients and sodium.

For the clearest stock, use an egg white to coagulate and trap fine particles in the liquid. After straining the stock the first time, lightly beat an egg white with ¼ cup cold water and stir into the stock. Bring to a boil, then remove from heat and let stand 5 minutes. Strain it again through a cheesecloth-lined sieve to remove the egg white and remaining particles.

SLOW-COOKER CHICKEN STOCK

This stock calls for whole chicken leg quarters, so it's a good one to make if you don't have a leftover chicken carcass. All it takes is 5 minutes of prep time and you get 10 cups of flavorful broth. *(Photo: page 222.)*

EQUIPMENT: 6-QUART SLOW COOKER

- 1 medium carrot, cut into 1-inch pieces
- 1 stalk celery, cut into 1-inch pieces
- 1 small onion, cut into 1-inch pieces
- 4 pounds skinless chicken leg quarters
- 6 sprigs fresh parsley
- 2 sprigs fresh thyme
- 1 bay leaf
- 1 clove garlic, crushed
- 20 whole black peppercorns
- 9 cups water

1. Combine carrot, celery, onion, chicken, parsley, thyme, bay leaf, garlic and peppercorns in a 6-quart slow cooker. Add water.

2. Cover and cook on High for 4 hours. Strain and let cool to room temperature.

➤➤ **MAKE AHEAD:** Refrigerate for up to 1 week or freeze for up to 3 months.

MAKES: ABOUT 10 CUPS

Analysis note: After straining, stock has negligible calories, nutrients and sodium.

ROASTED VEGETABLE STOCK

Roasting the vegetables along with a smear of tomato paste yields an extra-flavorful take on vegtable broth.

EQUIPMENT: 2 LARGE ROASTING PANS, STOCKPOT

- 6 large carrots, cut into 1-inch pieces
- 5 large onions, cut into 1-inch pieces
- 1 bulb fennel, cored and cut into 1-inch pieces
- 2 tablespoons canola oil
- 2 tablespoons tomato paste
- 1 cup white wine, divided
- 20 cups water
- 4 stalks celery, cut into 1-inch pieces
- ½ bunch parsley (about 10 sprigs)
- ½ bunch thyme (about 8 sprigs)
- 12 whole black peppercorns
- 6 cloves garlic, crushed and peeled
- 4 bay leaves

There's no need to peel the carrots before roasting—in fact, the skin adds flavor and color to the stock—but do give them a good scrubbing with a sturdy vegetable brush under cool running water.

1. Preheat oven to 425°F.

2. Combine carrots, onions and fennel in a large roasting pan. Toss with oil. Transfer half the vegetables to a second roasting pan. Roast the vegetables for 45 minutes, stirring every 15 minutes and switching the position of the pans each time you stir.

3. In one pan, push the vegetables to one side and spread tomato paste in the other side. Continue roasting (both pans) until the tomato paste begins to blacken, 15 minutes more.

4. Transfer the roasted vegetables to a large stockpot. Pour ½ cup wine into each roasting pan and bring to a boil over medium-high heat. Cook, scraping up any browned bits, for 1 to 2 minutes. Add the contents of the roasting pans to the stockpot, along with water, celery, parsley, thyme, peppercorns, garlic and bay leaves. Cover and bring to a simmer. Uncover and simmer for 1 hour without stirring, adjusting heat as necessary to maintain the simmer (if the stock boils it will become cloudy).

5. Strain the stock through a colander, pressing on the solids to remove all liquid. Discard the solids. Let the stock cool before storing.

▸▸ **MAKE AHEAD:** Refrigerate for up to 1 week or freeze for up to 3 months.

MAKES: 16 CUPS

Analysis note: After straining, stock has negligible calories, nutrients and sodium.

GARDEN VEGETABLE BROTH

This basic vegetable broth is made with fresh vegetables (as opposed to roasted) and has a bright, fresh taste. Use a variety of vegetables, depending on what you have. You can also use cut-up corn cobs or frozen vegetables. If adding strongly flavored vegetables to the mix, such as broccoli, Brussels sprouts, cabbage and cauliflower, use only a small amount.

EQUIPMENT: STOCKPOT

- 4 medium carrots *and/or* parsnips, scrubbed and sliced
- 3 medium onions *or* 4 leeks (white and light green parts only), coarsely chopped
- 3 stalks celery, chopped
- 2 cups mixed coarsely chopped vegetables, such as mushrooms, sweet potatoes, green beans, fennel, bell pepper *and/or* zucchini
- 3 cloves garlic, smashed
- ½ cup mixed fresh herbs, such as parsley, oregano, chives, basil, sage *and/or* tarragon
- 3 sprigs fresh thyme *or* 2 teaspoons dried
- 2 bay leaves
- 1 teaspoon salt
- ½ teaspoon whole black peppercorns
- 16 cups water

1. Combine carrots and/or parsnips, onions (or leeks), celery, mixed vegetables, garlic, mixed herbs, thyme, bay leaves, salt and peppercorns in a stockpot. Add water. Bring to a boil over high heat. Reduce heat to maintain a simmer and cook, uncovered, until the vegetables are soft and the stock is deeper in color, 1 to 1½ hours.

2. Line a colander with 2 layers of cheesecloth. Strain the stock and discard the solids. Let cool before storing.

▸▸ **MAKE AHEAD:** Refrigerate for up to 1 week or freeze for up to 3 months.

MAKES: 10 CUPS

Analysis note: After straining, stock has negligible calories, nutrients and sodium.

BEEF STOCK

This stock uses both beef and veal bones. The veal bones make it particularly rich and gelatinous. If you don't have them, substitute an equal amount of beef bones. The step of roasting the bones, which imparts fuller flavor, may be omitted if time is short.

EQUIPMENT: LARGE ROASTING PAN, STOCKPOT

- 3 pounds assorted beef bones (shin, shank, short ribs *or* marrow bones)
- 4 pounds veal bones
- 20 cups cold water
- 2 large onions, left whole
- 6 whole cloves
- 5 carrots, left whole
- 2 stalks celery, left whole
- 1 leek, white part only, rinsed thoroughly (see *Tip, page 197*)
- 1 large head garlic, unpeeled
- 5 sprigs fresh parsley
- 3 sprigs fresh thyme *or* ½ teaspoon dried
- 1 bay leaf

1. Preheat oven to 375°F. Place beef and veal bones in a large roasting pan. Roast until golden, 40 minutes.

2. Place the roasted bones in a large stockpot with water. Bring to a boil, skim foam and reduce heat to low. Stud each onion with 3 cloves. Add the onions, carrots, celery, leek, garlic, parsley, thyme and bay leaf to the pot. Simmer, uncovered, for 5 hours.

3. Strain through a fine sieve. Skim fat, if using immediately, or refrigerate overnight and remove solidified fat.

➤ **MAKE AHEAD:** Refrigerate for up to 1 week or freeze for up to 3 months.

MAKES: ABOUT 12 CUPS

Analysis note: After straining, stock has negligible calories, nutrients and sodium.

Marrow bones may make your stock a little cloudy, but the unctuous flavor is worth it.

AN ODE TO HOMEMADE STOCK

By Daniel Duane

My enduring love affair with soup stock began at Christmastime in 2005, when my mother asked me to make dinner for 24 members of our extended family. I happened to be hooked on a cookbook by Thomas Keller called *Bouchon*—a collection of recipes from his French bistro in the Napa Valley—so I picked a recipe called Braised Beef with Red Wine, or *Boeuf Bourguignon*. Like most Keller recipes, it required the preparation of multiple subrecipes located on different pages of the book, including one for veal stock.

I had never made any stock other than basic chicken, so I dutifully flipped to page 318 and made a shopping list that included 10 pounds of veal bones, two calves' feet, 16 ounces of tomato paste, a pound of leeks, two Spanish onions, two heads of garlic and a pound of tomatoes. It took a few phone calls to locate veal bones and calves' feet, but I finally got the goods and, back home, settled into an astonishingly involved process that began with first putting the bones and feet into a giant pot with lots of cold water, bringing it all slowly to a simmer over the course of an hour, pouring off all that water and replacing it with fresh, clean water, bringing that water slowly to a simmer over the course of an hour, then adding all the other ingredients and simmering for another 4 hours while skimming constantly.

I won't bore you with the details of the actual braised-beef recipe, except to say that it involved many more hours of work and an entire bottle of red wine, and that, on Christmas Day in my mother's kitchen, as our family waited in the dining room, it filled exactly 24 soup bowls with falling-apart-tender short rib, brightly colored baby onions and carrots, and a clear dark broth. Having forgotten that I was guest number 25, I sent out the last of those bowls with the horrified realization that nothing remained but a single cup of that broth in my big stockpot. So I poured the hot brown liquid into a mug and, hiding in a corner to protect my aunts and uncles from the worry that I was going without, I began to drink.

Anybody who has ever tasted a classically prepared *Bourguignon*, or even just a real-deal French veal stock properly seasoned, knows the soul-melting satisfaction that shivered through my being that evening, as my tongue and mouth recognized a mysteriously profound nourishment. Forgive me when I tell you that it felt like a revelation of ineluctable truth about human physiology—sort of like what happens to long-time vegetarians when they eat bacon.

In the years since, stock-making has become part of my domestic routine, a pleasurable chore that, like tidying up, feels vital to my well-being. There have been times of excess, to be sure, like the years when I took to buying whole lambs and pigs from local farmers, butchering them on my kitchen table and turning their skeletons—plus entire pigs' heads—into gallons upon gallons of lamb and pork stock, for the later preparation of endless soups and stews. There have been times of misguided obsession, too, like my pursuit of the ultimate ramen stock—inspired by David Chang's *Momofuku* cookbook—and my conclusion that serious ramen is one of those dishes so absurdly time-consuming, and so relatively inexpensive to buy premade, that sanity dictates leaving it to the pros. There have even been times of deliberate minimalism, when the only stock I made was Japanese *dashi*, albeit with rare seaweeds from Hokkaido and dried/fermented/smoked bonito that I shaved into fine flakes with a purpose-built Japanese tool called a *kezuriki*—all in the interest of a deadly serious miso soup. Most of all, though, the enduring lesson of that Christmas *Bourguignon* has been the unshakable knowledge that, as long as I have good stock on hand, I can deliver deliciousness to the people I love.

DANIEL DUANE *is a longtime contributor to* **Food & Wine,** *and the author of* How to Cook Like a Man: A Memoir of Cookbook Obsession.

BEEF BONE BROTH

Look for soup bones—including necks, shanks, knuckles, backs and marrow bones—at the meat department at your supermarket. (You may need to ask the butcher.) Be sure to roast the bones until they become very dark brown in color (almost burnt in some places) to give your broth the richest flavor and deepest color. To remove the most fat, refrigerate the broth overnight.

EQUIPMENT: 10- TO 12-QUART STOCKPOT

- 4 pounds beef soup bones
- 2 tablespoons extra-virgin olive oil
- 4 medium carrots, cut into 2-inch pieces
- 4 stalks celery (with leaves), cut into 3-inch pieces
- 2 medium onions, quartered
- 2 medium tomatoes, halved
- 1 head garlic, halved crosswise
- 16 cups cold water, divided
- 2 tablespoons cider vinegar
- 2 sprigs thyme
- 2 bay leaves
- 1 tablespoon whole black peppercorns
- 1 tablespoon kosher salt

Adding a splash of vinegar to stock or broth before it starts simmering helps to break down collagen in the bones, which releases more gelatin. The additional gelatin improves the body, texture and flavor of the stock.

1. Arrange racks in upper and lower thirds of oven; preheat to 400°F.

2. Place soup bones on a rimmed baking sheet and drizzle with oil. Roast on the bottom rack for 30 minutes.

3. Combine carrots, celery, onions, tomatoes and garlic on a second rimmed baking sheet. Move the bones to the upper rack and place the vegetables on the lower rack. Roast until the bones are deep brown and the vegetables are starting to brown in spots, 30 to 45 minutes more.

4. Transfer the bones and vegetables to a 10- to 12-quart stockpot. Add 1 cup water to the bone pan and scrape up any browned bits with a wooden spoon; add to the pot. Add the remaining 15 cups water, vinegar, thyme, bay leaves, peppercorns and salt. Cover and bring to a boil over high heat. Reduce heat to maintain a low simmer and cook, covered, for 8 hours.

5. Remove the bones (if desired, remove any meat from the bones and save for another use). Strain the broth through a large sieve into a large bowl; discard the solids. Skim fat from the surface, if desired.

▸▸ **MAKE AHEAD:** Refrigerate for up to 1 week or freeze for up to 3 months.

MAKES: 10 CUPS

Analysis note: After straining, broth has negligible calories, nutrients and sodium.

FISH STOCK

Fish stock is sometimes hard to find at the supermarket. Besides looking for shelf-stable ones, scout out the freezer for frozen stock with other seafood. If you make this one, you'll need to seek out heads and bones at the fish counter of your grocery store or at a fish market.

EQUIPMENT: STOCKPOT

3	pounds white fish heads and bones
2	cups dry white wine
2	onions, chopped
2	leeks, white parts only, cleaned and chopped *(see Tip, page 197)*
2	stalks celery, chopped
2	cloves garlic, crushed
4	sprigs fresh parsley
3	sprigs fresh thyme *or* ½ teaspoon dried
1	bay leaf
12-14	cups cold water

1. Rinse fish heads and bones in cool water and place in a nonaluminum stockpot. Add wine, onions, leeks, celery, garlic, parsley, thyme and bay leaf. Add enough cold water to cover. Bring just to a boil. Reduce heat to low, skim off any foam and simmer, uncovered, for 30 to 35 minutes, skimming occasionally.

2. Strain stock through a fine sieve. Let cool before storing.

➤ **MAKE AHEAD:** Refrigerate for up to 1 week or freeze for up to 3 months.

MAKES: ABOUT 12 CUPS

Analysis note: After straining, stock has negligible calories, nutrients and sodium.

SOUP-MAKING PANTRY STAPLES

Keeping a few ingredients on hand means you can whip up a pot of soup anytime. See what we keep stocked to help throw together a meal without leaving your house.

PANTRY

Broth: low-sodium chicken, beef, mushroom, "no-chicken" *and/or* vegetable

Dried herbs

Spices

Canned tomatoes

Tomato paste

Reduced-sodium soy sauce

Salsa

Whole-wheat pasta

Brown rice

Barley

Quinoa

Wild rice

Bulgur

Farro

Canned *or* dried beans

Shelf-stable tofu

Garlic

Potatoes

Onions

Olive oil

Vinegar

Peanut butter

REFRIGERATOR

Celery

Carrots

Miso

Hot sauce

Sesame oil

Nonfat *or* low-fat milk

Lemons & limes

Parmesan cheese

Yogurt

FREEZER

Broccoli

Corn

Edamame

Lima beans

Chopped onions

Pearl onions

Peas

Spinach

Stir-fry mix

FREEZER SMARTS

When it comes to saving food, freezers are our best friends. And if you know before you cook that you're going to freeze, you may want to do things a little differently. Here are some handy tips and tricks to make sure your frozen soup tastes as delicious as the day it was made.

PORTION IT OUT

Turn your big batch of soup into convenient grab-and-go meals by freezing in individual servings. Use quart-size freezer bags or 4-cup freezer-safe plastic or glass containers to accommodate a couple of servings while giving the soup room to expand as it freezes.

COOL IT DOWN

Putting hot soup directly in the freezer can thaw your frozen food. Place hot soup pot in an ice-water bath in your sink and stir often. To speed up the process, divide soup into smaller portions before cooling.

SEPARATE GRAINS AND PASTA

Pasta and grains soak up liquid and soften a bit as they freeze, so you may want to add more broth before serving. If you like them al dente, cook and freeze pasta and grains separately from the soup.

KEEP VEGETABLES AL DENTE

Cook vegetables until just tender and still a bit crisp. They'll be perfect for your bowl for dinner and they'll stay firm when frozen and reheated.

HOLD THE DAIRY

Dairy tends to separate and become grainy when frozen and reheated. Leave it out of the soup and write on the container how much to add after reheating so you don't have to root around for the recipe later on.

LABEL, LABEL, LABEL

Food can disappear into a freezer like it's in the Bermuda Triangle. To minimize the mystery, label soups with the recipe name, the date it was made and reheating and garnishing instructions so you remember where you left off.

SAVE THE GARNISH

Leave garnishes, such as chopped fresh herbs or nuts, off before freezing. When frozen, herbs lose their oomph and nuts lose their crunch.

HOW TO FOLLOW AN EATINGWELL RECIPE

Once we're sure the recipe works well, it's up to you to follow the recipe. It's important to keep in mind a few simple guidelines and tips for how to read our recipes.

THE INGREDIENT LIST

The comma matters. When we call for ingredients, pay attention to where the comma is because it can have a significant effect on what we're calling for.

Here are some examples:
- "1 pound chicken, trimmed" means we are calling for 1 pound purchased chicken and then you trim it.
- "1 cup nuts, chopped" means we are calling for 1 cup of nuts and then you chop them. "1 cup chopped nuts," on the other hand, means you should chop your nuts and then measure out 1 cup of them.
- "1 cup frozen corn, thawed" means we are calling for 1 cup of frozen corn and then you thaw it. On the other hand, "1 cup thawed frozen corn" means that you thaw first and then measure.

Word order matters too. The action closest to the ingredient happens first: to get "1 cup diced peeled potato" (reading right to left), you'll peel the potato, then dice and measure.

Market quantities versus measures. We aim to make shopping as easy as possible, so we usually call for market quantities of ingredients rather than measures.
- For example, a market quantity would be 1 small onion, while a measure would be ¾ cup diced onion. When we call for a measure it is typically because we think that using the specified amount of the ingredient is important to the outcome of the recipe.

TIPS FOR MEASURING

Measuring accurately when cooking and baking is one of the best ways to guarantee successful results in the kitchen. In the *EatingWell* Test Kitchen, we use four types of standard U.S. measuring tools:

DRY MEASURING CUPS Metal or plastic measuring cups, usually sold in a set, that are available in ¼-, ⅓-, ½-, ¾- and 1-cup sizes. Dry ingredients, such as flour and grains, should be measured in dry measuring cups.

LIQUID MEASURING CUPS Clear glass or plastic cups with pour spouts that are available in 1-, 2-, 4- and 8-cup sizes and have measurements marked on the side of the cup. When measuring liquids, place a clear liquid measuring cup on a level surface. Pour in the liquid, then verify the measure by looking at it from eye level, not from above.

MEASURING SPOONS Small spoons in ¼-, ½-, 1-teaspoon and 1-tablespoon sizes designed to measure small quantities of dry or liquid ingredients. When a teaspoon or tablespoon measure is called for in a recipe, we don't mean the regular silverware spoons you eat with.

KITCHEN SCALE Although it is not necessary to have a kitchen scale to make our recipes, a small digital scale that can measure up to at least 5 pounds is a handy tool to have in the kitchen to ensure accuracy.

KNIFE SKILLS

How you cut ingredients is important; it helps to distribute the ingredient throughout the dish (mincing or finely chopping garlic, for example), ensure that ingredients cook at the same time (like cutting carrots and potatoes into 1-inch dice) or improve texture (a thinly sliced piece of smoked salmon, for example, is more tempting on your bagel than a fat chunk). Pay attention to, but don't stress about, these terms. Your common sense will go a long way in helping as you cook.

MINCE & FINELY CHOP "Mincing" is the finest chop of all, less than ⅛ inch, achieved by cutting, then rocking the knife back and forth across the ingredients, while rotating the blade around on the cutting board. "Finely chop" is a little larger than mince.

CHOP & COARSELY CHOP You want to wind up with about a ½- to 1-inch piece when you chop, a bit larger when you "coarsely chop." The idea of chopping (unlike dicing) is that the ingredients don't have to be uniform in shape.

DICE & CUBE You're aiming for uniformity of size here. Most recipes that call for a "dice" or "cube" will indicate the preferred size for cooking in the time allotted (e.g., "cut into

1-inch cubes"). Ignore these measurements and you will alter the cooking time.

SLICE & THINLY SLICE "Slice" is a judgment call, but if you insist on a general rule, think of a slice no thinner than ¼ inch. "Thinly slice," however, means you will want to cut the food as thinly as possible. This will vary by ingredient: you can slice an apple to near-transparent thinness, which is hard to do with steak.

SLICE DIAGONALLY Also known as slicing "on the bias," this is just like slicing, but instead of making a perpendicular cut you cut on an angle. It's an attractive way to cut long vegetables, such as scallions, celery and zucchini. To slice diagonally, hold the knife at a 45-degree angle to the vegetable and then cut it.

CUT INTO JULIENNE Also known as matchstick cut: food is cut into long thin strips. To get a matchstick, first slice the vegetable and then trim the edges to get even rectangles (about 1 to 2 inches long). Then stack the rectangles and slice lengthwise into matchsticks.

HOW WE TEST *and* ANALYZE RECIPES

At *EatingWell* we aim to create recipes that work perfectly and taste absolutely delicious. They also adhere to guidelines for healthful eating. To that end, we rigorously test each recipe we publish—and then provide accurate nutritional information so you can make informed decisions about what you eat. Here's how we do it.

HOW WE TEST RECIPES

■ Recipes are tested on multiple times by different testers—both home cooks and culinary school graduates.

■ We test on gas and electric stoves.

■ We use a variety of tools and techniques.

■ Testers shop major supermarkets to research availability of ingredients.

■ Testers measure active and total time to prepare each recipe.

■ "Active" time includes prep time (the time it takes to chop, dice, puree, mix, combine, etc., before cooking begins), but it also includes the time spent tending something on the stovetop, in the oven or on the grill—and getting it to the table. If you can't walk away from it, we consider it active minutes.

■ "Total" includes both active and inactive minutes and indicates the entire amount of time required for each recipe, start to finish.

■ "Make Ahead" gives storage instructions to help you plan. If particular "Equipment" is needed, we tell you that at the top of the recipe.

HOW WE ANALYZE RECIPES

■ All recipes are analyzed for nutrition content by a registered dietitian.

■ We analyze for calories, total fat, saturated (sat) fat, cholesterol, carbohydrate, total sugars, added sugars, protein, fiber, sodium and potassium using The Food Processor® SQL Nutrition Analysis Software from ESHA Research, Salem, Oregon.

■ When a recipe gives a measurement range of an ingredient, we analyze the first amount.

■ When alternative ingredients are listed, we analyze the first one suggested.

■ Garnishes and optional ingredients are not included in analyses.

■ We do not include trimmings or marinade that is not absorbed.

■ Recipes are tested and analyzed with iodized table salt unless otherwise indicated.

■ We estimate that rinsing with water reduces the sodium in canned foods by 35 percent. (Readers on sodium-restricted diets can reduce or eliminate the salt in a recipe.)

■ To help people eat in accordance with the USDA's Dietary Guidelines, *EatingWell*'s suggested portions generally are based upon standard serving sizes. For example, suggested servings for meat, poultry and fish are generally 3 to 4 ounces, cooked. A recommended portion of a starch, such as rice or potatoes, is generally ½ cup.

■ When a recipe provides 20 percent or more of the Daily Value (dv) of a nutrient, it is listed as a nutrition bonus. These values are FDA benchmarks for adults eating 2,000 calories a day.

For more on our nutritional-analysis process, visit *eatingwell. com/go/guidelines*.

WHAT OUR DIETARY TAGS MEAN

The recipes in this book (at least the ones that deserve it) are tagged at the top of the page as Low-Calorie and/or Heart-Healthy and/or Vegetarian and/or Gluten-Free. (For full lists of recipes that meet the criteria, see the Special-Interest Indexes on page 252.)

LOW-CALORIE

Nutrition parameters for *EatingWell* recipes are based on a 2,000-calorie diet, an intake level that is appropriate for an average healthy person who is trying to maintain a healthy weight. Recipes that qualify as Low-Calorie are consistent with a 1,500-calorie-per-day diet (indicating a 25 percent total calorie reduction per day), an intake level that enables most people to lose a healthy 1 to 2 pounds per week.
■ Entrees: Calories ≤375 per serving
■ Combo meals: Calories ≤575 per serving
■ Side dishes: Calories ≤200 per serving

HEART-HEALTHY

To receive a Heart-Healthy tag, recipes must meet the following thresholds per serving:
■ Entrees: Saturated fat ≤2-4 grams / Sodium ≤360 mg
■ Combo meals: Saturated fat ≤4-6 grams / Sodium ≤600 mg
■ Side dishes: Saturated fat ≤2 grams / Sodium ≤240 mg

Recommendations are based on the guidelines for the American Heart Association (AHA) Heart-Check program and general recommendations for reduced saturated fat (≤5-6% of total calories) and reduced sodium (≤1,500 mg/day).

VEGETARIAN

Meatless (i.e., no meat, poultry or seafood) or includes meatless options (such as a soup that calls for chicken broth or vegetable broth) and contains no ingredients derived from meat-based products (e.g., gelatin, animal-based broths, fish sauce, oyster sauce). These recipes may still include eggs, egg products, butter and milk or other dairy-containing ingredients.

GLUTEN-FREE

Does not contain wheat, barley or rye or any ingredient that contains or is derived from one of these ingredients (e.g., triticale, spelt, kamut, wheat bran, durum flour, enriched flour, semolina). Recipes marked as gluten-free call for tamari (versus soy sauce) and gluten-free oats (instead of regular oats).
Check the labels of processed foods, such as broths and condiments, to make sure they don't contain hidden sources of gluten.

INDEX

Page numbers in *italics* refer to photos.

SPECIAL-INTEREST INDEXES

For more information, see "What Our Dietary Tags Mean," page 239. (Page numbers in *italics* refer to photos.)

GLUTEN-FREE

HEART-HEALTHY

LOW-CALORIE

VEGETARIAN

VEGAN

*Vegan recipes omit all animal-based
products (e.g., meat, poultry, fish, milk
and eggs) and ingredients from animal
sources (e.g., butter, lard, gelatin, fish
sauce, oyster sauce, Worcestershire
sauce, animal-based broths, honey, etc.).*

CONTRIBUTORS

Bruce Aidells: Singapore-Style Chicken & Noodle Soup, 71; Portuguese Kale & Red Bean Soup, 141; Spanish Chickpea Soup, 178

John Ash: Old-Fashioned Winter Vegetable Chowder, 150

Nancy Baggett: Sweet Potato-Peanut Bisque, 100

Lidia Bastianich: Ribollita, 50

Sara Stillman Berger: Norma's Mushroom Barley Soup, 63

David Bonom: Bean & Barley Soup, 131; Tofu & Vegetable Soup, 149; Homemade Roasted Chicken Stock, 225

Lisa Holderness Brown: Italian Bread & Tomato Soup, 36; Smoky Chicken-Chile Soup with Tamale Dumplings, 46; Pot Roast Soup, 68; Chunky Cheeseburger Soup, 99; Cuban Black Bean Soup, 134; Sopa Tarasca, 142; Mulligatawny Soup, 170; Lamb & Root Vegetable Stew with Gremolata, 181; Garden Vegetable Broth, 228

Carolyn Casner: Loaded Baked Potato Soup, 104; Chicken Soups by the Formula, 211–213; Chowders by the Formula, 214–217

Danielle Centoni: Roasted Cauliflower & Potato Curry Soup, 49; Thai Coconut Curry Soup, 60; Kielbasa & Cabbage Soup, 67; Four-Bean & Pumpkin Chili, 137

Julia Clancy: Spring Lima Bean Soup with Crispy Bacon, 132

Natalie Danford: Chicken Soup with Passatelli, 103; White Bean & Vegetable Soup, 128

Sarah DiGregorio: Faux Chicken Pho, 121; Miso Soup with Shrimp & Green Tea Soba, 122; Coconut Curry with Butternut Squash Noodles, 123; Sichuan Ramen with Cabbage & Tofu, 124

Sarah Fritschner: Soup Beans, 135

Chef Jesús González, Rancho La Puerta: Spicy Butternut Squash Soup, 40

Patricia Green & Carolyn Hemming: Quinoa Peanut Soup (Sopa de Mani), 146

Kathy Gunst: Roasted Cauliflower Soup with Parsley-Chive Swirl, 193; Roasted Pumpkin Soup with Glazed Pepitas, 194; New Mexico Green Chile & Pork Stew, 201; Matzo Ball Soup with Fresh Dill, 202; Winter Vegetable Soup with Turkish Meatballs, 206

Joyce Hendley: Veggistrone, 54; Southwestern Vegetable & Chicken Soup, 163; Borscht with Beef, 164; Moroccan Lentil Soup, 177

Susan Herr: Orange & Saffron-Scented Mussel Soup, 153

Emily Horton: Creamy Rye & Butternut Squash Soup, 22

Raghavan Iyer: Paprika & Red Pepper Soup with Pistachios, 33

Patsy Jamieson: Turkish Chickpea & Lamb Soup, 72

Cheryl & Bill Jamison: Grilled Tomato Gazpacho, 32

Barbara Kafka: Amazing Pea Soup, 41

Breana Lai: Mexican Cabbage Soup, 45; Cucumber-Almond Gazpacho, 59; Cheese Toasts, 92–93; French Onion Soup, 182; Breadsticks, 186–187

Carolyn Malcoun: Tomato Soup, 35; Chipotle Albondigas Soup, 64; Italian Egg-Drop Soup, 159; Potato-Leek Bisque, 197; Roasted Vegetable Stock, 227; Slow-Cooker Chicken Stock, 226

Ivy Manning: Celeriac & Apple Soup with Blue Cheese Toasts, 21; Winter Vegetable Dal, 138; Quinoa Mushroom Soup, 198

Hilary Meyer: Chilled Strawberry-Rhubarb Soup, 19

Devon O'Brien: Shrimp & Kimchi Noodle Soup, 118; Spicy Ramen with Mushrooms & Spinach, 119; Chicken Curry Zoodle Soup, 120

Ellen Ecker Ogden: Fragrant Fish Soup, 154

Annie Peterson: Jerusalem Artichoke-Potato Soup with Crispy Croutons, 25; Arugula-Zucchini Vichyssoise, 87; Green Gazpacho, 91; Chicken Potpie Soup with Tater Tot Topping, 96; Green Eggs & Ham Soup, 107; Squish-Squash Mac & Cheese Soup, 108; Creamy Tomato Soup with Tortellini, 111; Chicken Enchilada Soup, 112; Chicken-Corn Tortilla Soup, 168; Lentil & Root Veggie Soup, 174; Beef Bone Broth, 231

Jim Romanoff: Crab Bisque with Avocado, Tomato & Corn Relish, 155; Swedish Yellow Split Pea Soup with Ham, 173; Shiitake & Noodle Hot & Sour Soup, 185

Scott Rosenbaum: Plantain Soup (Sopa de Platanos), 97

Christine Burns Rudalevige: Smoked Gouda-Broccoli Soup, 39

Bill Scepansky: Maryland Oyster Stew, 18

Marie Simmons: Celery & Parmesan Minestrone, 160

Lesley Téllez: Caldo Tlalpeño (Mexican Chicken Soup), 42

Anna Thomas: Basic Green Soup, 76; Very Green Lentil Soup, 79; Spinach & Goat Cheese Bisque, 80; Green Curry Soup, 83; Green Soup with Yams & Sage, 84; Rustic Parsley & Orzo Soup with Walnuts, 88

Cathy Whims: Wild Mushroom Soup, 29

Katie Workman: Chicken, Barley & Mushroom Soup, 205

Grace Young: Shrimp & Chinese Chive Wonton Soup, 26